Killer Gold Digger Molly Corbett

Ana Benton

Published by Trellis Publishing, 2021.

KILLER GOLD DIGGER MOLLY CORBETT

First edition. July 9, 2021.

Copyright © 2021 Ana Benton.

ISBN: 979-8224383511

Written by Ana Benton.

KILLER GOLD DIGGER : THE TRUE STORY OF MOLLY CORBETT

ANA BENTON

BRANDY HOLMES

It was New Year's Day in 2003 when retired pastor Julian Brandon heard a knock on his door in Blanchard, Louisiana. He opened it to find the villainous duo of Brandy Holmes and Robert Coleman who "bum rushed" the 70-year old man, forcing their way in.

The couple shot the minister and began ransacking his home.

His wife, Alice, tried hiding in the back bedroom but Brandy and Coleman followed her, demanding valuables before shooting her.

They then stole whatever they could out of the home; cash, credit cards, and jewelry.

Brandy would only be captured after she bragged to one of her neighbors that she killed an elderly couple.

She would be sentenced to death but would blame being born with fetal alcohol syndrome for her behavior. By doing this, she could avoid personal responsibility, as her life was filled with murder and mayhem.

"I was named after my mother's favorite drink," she said. "Brandy."

Born out of a childhood of neglect and growing anger, Brandy Holmes would become one of the most vicious killers in Louisiana history.

EARLY LIFE

Brandy's mother, Brenda Bruce, would drink whiskey through the first three months of her pregnancy before switching to beer. She would give birth to Brenda Aileen Holmes on July 25th, 1979 in Tylertown, Mississippi.

Brenda and her common-law husband Johnny Holmes would separate early in Brandy's life, however. Brenda would then take the two-year-old Brandy and leave for Shreveport, Louisiana. Brandy would be neglected by Brenda throughout her younger years as her mother would battle her own alcoholism addiction as well as having to deal with two other children from a previous union.

As the product of a neglectful home, Brandy began acting out. This would not be documented until she entered elementary school where she became an immediate discipline problem. Inside the school, she yelled at teachers, ate rocks in the schoolyard and was soon placed into special education classes. Her out of control behavior would not be limited to school as one day when she returned home, she killed a kitten.

At the age of twelve, Brenda would claim that Brandy was raped. She would then be institutionalized at Sand Hill Hospital in Mississippi for six months. Psychiatrists would later state that Brandy had the mental function of a seventh grader and had no empathy for other people.

She would drop out of school in the sixth grade. By the age of thirteen, Brandy was running with a "black street gang" and participated in drive-by shootings. She would be expelled from school after bringing knives to class.

Now free from academic obligations, Brandy would embark on a crime career full-time, committing small-time thefts and home burglaries. On one occasion, she and a boyfriend tried to kidnap a girl in Mississippi in the hopes of holding her for ransom. In and out of juvenile hall, her disdain for authority would manifest itself in numerous occasions as she fought with corrections officers. In one instance, she got a hold of a piece of broken glass and cut the throat of one of the officers.

"Brandy had a pathological dislike for anyone in authority," forensic psychiatrist Gil White said. "She had spent her entire life in and out of juvenile hall. This would mean daily encounters with fellow inmates who were just as evil and malicious as she was. But she always made it a point to do them one better. There was one inmate who would taunt Brandy at the corrections facility on a daily basis. Brandy knew that her harasser would come at her at only certain times during the day. So she got a bottle of acid and waited for the girl to come into her cell. The taunts began and Brandy threw the acid into the young woman's face. Her victim screamed as the acid burned into her eyes and face. Brandy would only laugh in satisfaction."

Brandy would be continuously incarcerated for most of her life, never holding a job. She had an IQ of 77 but still plotted out elaborate burglaries, knowing how to "police" herself afterward by not leaving behind fingerprints or evidence.

"Brandy talked as if she were 'black'," White said. "She mimicked the voice and cadence of someone who grew up in a black ghetto. The majority of her friends were black and she embraced the culture of ghetto crime early on. She loved committing crimes and then bragging about them to anyone who would listen."

She would break and enter homes until her another arrest got her a juvenile prison sentence for six years until she turned twenty-one. Once again, she would fight correctional officers at the Jetson Correctional Center for youth and would be sentenced as an adult to the Louisiana Correctional Institute for Women.

"Brandy's reputation around the jail had reached the warden," White said. "The warden would comment on how she had been unable to break down Brandy. That is how incorrigible she was. Her behavior had stood out to someone who had seen everything over a period of decades. But the one person she would single out as being 'tough' was Brandy Holmes."

She would be released at the age of twenty-three but only more mayhem would await. She had remained out of jail for over seven months but her criminal mind started to each. Brandy began to think bigger in terms of obtaining that adrenaline rush in committing a crime.

GETTING BOLDER

During Christmas Eve of 2002, Brandy would visit her father Johnny in Tylertown, Mississippi. He lived near the dubious "Cloud Nine" neighborhood which was one of the most violent-prone in the state. It was a biracial community with a lot of drugs and shootings among the numerous mobile homes.

Brandy felt right at home in the "Cloud Nine" neighborhood as she visited her father's trailer on the pretense of a visit. But what she really wanted was his gun.

She watched as her father shot the gun off during a celebration and noted where he kept the weapon for safekeeping.

When he wasn't looking, Brandy took the .380 caliber handgun and returned to Louisiana.

She hooked up with her boyfriend, Robert Coleman upon arriving back home. Coleman was an African-American man with a long history of criminal behavior. He walked with a perpetual scowl and victimized people of all skin colors.

"Robert was ten years older than Brandy," White said. "She saw him as a kind of hero as he did things she always wanted to do but didn't have the muscle or nerve."

They became a crime duo, robbing other gang members and committing petty thefts.

Now armed with a .380 caliber gun, Brandy got a little bolder than usual.

During a New Year's celebration at her mother's home, Brenda asked everyone what their New Year's resolution was. Without hesitation, Brandy pulled out the gun from her purse.

"I'm about to 'hit a lick.'" Brandy said, kissing Coleman.

"Hitting or jacking a lick," White said. "Meant that she was going to commit a crime of some sort. Probably a robbery. But everyone at the party was probably so drunk or high they didn't care."

Robert Coleman, however, took Brandy seriously. He saw the gun as a tool for them to commit more crimes.

"That's why she was drawn to Robert," White said. "He was described by one detective as one of the most callous human beings she had ever encountered. That's what drew Brandy to him. Plus, he accepted her in ways that the upstanding young men in the community didn't. Brandy was overweight with a bulbous forehead and a mean facial expression. Her potential suitors were not church-going college students. Her suitors, and she didn't have a lot, were bad people. Men like Robert Coleman."

LET THE STALKING BEGIN

Looking for people to rob, Brandy would enter a gated community called "Nob Hill", a place for elderly residents. Seemingly picking out a house at random, Brandy knocked on the door of Patricia Camp.

"Hi there," she said. "Is Theresa McGee here?"

"I'm sorry," Camp said. "There's no one here by that name."

Thinking she had an easy target, Brandy enlisted the aid of her boyfriend Robert Coleman and returned to Camp's residence. The two knocked on the door and Brandy asked if she could use the phone.

Now suspicious, Camp refused and closed the door.

If she had let the duo into her home she would have robbed and most likely murdered.

A VICTIM BY CHANCE

On New Years Day, Brandy decided that she would visit the grave of a friend in a rural town called Blanchard.

Blanchard was a relatively peaceful and quiet rural area with a population of less than 3,000. Violent robberies and murders simply did not happen there.

Until Brandy Holmes decided to pay a visit.

While mourning over her friend's gravestone, she noticed an elderly couple that lived behind the graveyard. Brandy watched from behind the headstones as the married man and wife performed their gardening duties.

They were old. They were vulnerable. They probably had money considering they had the biggest house in the neighborhood.

They were the Julian and Alice Brandon, known to most everyone in town as the nicest people around town. People who would give you the shirt off their back.

"They were well-loved at church and in the community," White said. "They were getting ready to celebrate their fiftieth wedding anniversary."

Brandy then contacted her partner in crime, Robert Coleman, and told him of the couple she had spotted near the graveyard.

"Time to hit a lick," she told Coleman when she came home. "I found the perfect couple. They are as weak as kittens!"

This go around, Brandy made a necessary adjustment to her ruse. She would not make the same mistake she did with Patricia Camp by being too polite. This time, she would not use the pretense of looking for a person who didn't live there or ask to use the telephone.

She would use Coleman's muscle to force their way inside.

Lounging around their home in the early evening, Julian and Alice sipped hot cocoa while watching a television program.

Then came a knock at the door. They weren't expecting anyone this late in the evening and Alice looked concerned.

"I'll see who it is," Julian got up and went to the door.

Opening up, he was forced out back into the home by the gun-toting Robert Coleman.

Brandy barged in and watched as Coleman placed the handgun under the Pastor's jaw and fired.

The bullet separated into two pieces, one fragment entered his brain while the other exited the top of his head and into the dining room ceiling.

Blood splattered on the wall as Pastor Julian fell to the ground.

Brandy and Coleman then grabbed Alice. They dragged her to the back bedroom and demanded everything she had. Cash, credit cards, and jewelry.

"Brandy and Coleman were devils," White said. "Monsters. They shot Julian almost immediately upon entering the home. Alice didn't know what to do. It was like a nightmare come to life. They grabbed her and demanded credit cards. ATM cards. They demanded to know the PIN numbers."

The 68-year old woman begged for her life but the two demons would not hear it.

"Oh, Sweet Jesus!" Alice screamed. "Oh, Sweet Jesus, please don't shoot me!"

Alice's hysterics made Brandy anxious. The monster then placed a pillow over the elderly woman's head and ordered Coleman to shoot her.

They returned to the dining room and to their amazement, saw the Reverend Julian struggling to get up.

Brandy then went to the kitchen and found three Chicago Cutlery knives in the drawer. She and Coleman then began stabbing the Reverend to death. They would slice at his nose and face then stab him in his head and chest.

"They were each trying to upstage the other," White said. "Brandy was trying to show Robert what a 'bad ass' she was by stabbing the old man. He, in turn, enjoyed the admiration he received from Brandy. He liked doing 'evil shit' in order to gain her worship."

They would then cut the Reverend's throat two times, a slicing would that encircled his entire neck, severing his carotid artery and jugular vein.

Brandy then left one of the knives embedded in Pastor Julian's back, six-inches deep.

Their handiwork done, Brandy "policed" the place, wiping for fingerprints as well as removing the bullet casings from the floor and the ceiling. But it was all futile as the two left bloody footprints all over the house.

Brandy would then take the Reverend's ATM card and try to withdraw cash. When that failed, Brandy burned the card and tossed it in the woods behind her mother's trailer along with the gun.

She then tried to pawn off the jewelry to a neighbor. The neighbor described Brandy as taking pleasure in showing him the wedding rings, gold bracelets, and other valuables. He then asked where she got all of the jewelry and she bragged "I killed some old people.

The neighbor scoffed at the answer which seemed to make the insecure Brandy angry. She wanted to be seen as a 'bad ass'.

Two days later, Brandy would take her nephews to the Brandon residence. She would enter the home with one of her nephews (a 9-year old) and upon making too much noise in the house they would hear Alice screaming for help in the back bedroom. Both of her nephews would sprint away from the residence while Brandy would remain in the home.

MORE MAYHEM

Wanting that same adrenaline high, the couple would seek out a gang member friend named Terrance Blaze. Blaze would get inside their vehicle in the front passenger side seat with Coleman driving. Brandy, sitting in the backseat, would shoot Blaze in the head at point-blank range. They would then dump the body near her mother's trailer.

"Blaze was a friend of theirs," White said. "He was twenty-five years old. They killed him simply for the thrill of it. There was no motive involved in the killing of Terrance Blaze. This was a case of them not wanting to experience the same high of killing the Brandon couple. They had to kill again and Terrance was a convenient target."

THE DISCOVERY

The brutalized couple would not be found until January 5th, 2003, four days later. Calvin Hudson was a family friend of the Brandons and became concerned when the couple did not come to church that Sunday. He went to check on them and found Pastor Julian lying in a pool of his own blood on the carpet. Panicked, Hudson went to a neighbor's home and police were called.

Amazingly, they discovered that Alice Brandon was still alive. Medical personnel was called and they arranged for a helicopter to come and medivac Alice to the hospital as the house was in a rural part of the parish.

The details of the horrific crime made the news and the Caddo Parish Sheriff's Office would receive tips from people who lived at an apartment complex near the Brandon residence. One of them included the man whom Brandy tried to sell off Alice's jewelry.

Obtaining their identification, police converged on the trailer of Brandy's mother, Brenda Bruce. Inside, they would find Brandy, Coleman and Brandy's 15-year-old brother, Sean George.

Inside the trailer, investigators would find a multi-colored bracelet that belonged to Alice Brandon. A box of food service gloves were found which had a diamond pattern consistent with the blood transfer stains found at the murder scene. Also, three fired .380 cartridge casings were found in the gutter of the trailer. These casings would later much the casings found on Brandy's father's property when he had fired the gun into a tree prior to it being stolen.

THE INTERROGATION

The detectives found Brandy to be a willing informant after some initial resistance. They had her remove her shoes as they knew it would match the bloody footprints they found at the Brandon residence. Brandy knew she had been caught dead to rights and she also couldn't resist the opportunity to tell the detectives about her crimes.

"I can show you where I threw their credit cards," she said. "But then I'd have to show you something else. A dead body. "

She was informed of her Miranda rights and told them about the body of Terrance Blaze without any prompting.

"Brandy came from a prison culture where everyone got an ego boost as they talked about the crimes they committed," White said. "The more horrific the crime, the bigger the rep. So Brandy could not resist the ego boost that she thought she could get by telling the detective about her crimes, in essence, she was bragging about them to the interrogator. Her need to feel validated trumped her need to not incriminate herself."

The detective then put his guard down and left Brandy alone at the desk. She realized that the videotape recorder had filmed her entire confession. Seizing the opportunity, Brandy took the tape from inside the camera and replaced it with a blank one she found on the detective's desk. He returned and she asked to go to the bathroom. She then flushed the tape down the toilet.

Police would discover the ruse and were still able to prosecute Brandy without her taped confession.

While incarcerated, Brandy did not take the whole process seriously. Her attorneys noted that she didn't seem to fully understand the extent of the punishment she was about to receive. Her letter to a friend after her arrest reflects her mindset at the time.

"Hey Chaz,

I know you thought I forgot about you. No Never that Honey. I'm Back locked up if you didn't see it on the news or in the newspaper. Girl, yes. They got me charged with 1st degree murder armed robbery attempted 1 st degree murder and 2nd degree murder. I sit there and watched my Baby's Daddy kill these white folks and yes I took the Visa card the gold Mastercard and the codes and cleaned there Bank accounts out. They was going to Book my 15 year old Brother, But I went ahead and took all charges & I have Affidavit to get notarized so I can let my Baby's daddy go to[o]. You know damn well I'm going to try my Best to escape and you know this too. I got it mostly planned. Don't be mad, Chaz. I gotta have my Money ya know. I goes back to court Feb. 18th 03 Girl don't worry yourself about me. I'll be okay, I guess you know. You be cool and write me back and tell me the low down/who all is Back up in there okay.

Here's my address okay .

Love Always,Ms. Brandy"

Her letter above was admitted as evidence. It would be used to show that Brandy had forethought when she committed her crimes.

"But for Brandy and Robert meeting each other, they both would have probably been limited to burglaries and incarceration," White said. "But the both of them together was like a match to dynamite. The crimes would have escalated and they would have hurt a lot of people."

Alice Brandon, the lone survivor of Brandy's rampage, would be comatose for several years before finally passing away in October of 2008. Alice would be disabled for the rest of his life and required the insertion of feeding and tracheotomy tubes.

In 2005, both Coleman and Brandy would be convicted of first-degree murder. Brandy is one of only two women who are on Louisiana's death row.

MOLLY CORBETT

Some criminal cases truly divide the public, and the murder of a wealthy Irish businessman Jason Corbett was certainly one of them. He was viciously killed by his second wife Molly Corbett and her father Thomas. Even though the killers claimed that it was self-defense because Jason tried to strangle Molly, the evidence spoke a different story. It was clearly a planned killing that had a different goal – securing Molly with the life insurance money and gaining the custody of Jason's children. She met Jason while she worked as an au pair and got very attached to the youngsters.

The police conducted a thorough investigation that shocked everyone involved. It was clear that the murder was personal and that Molly got rid of Jason in a most horrific way because he wanted to leave her and move back to Ireland. She couldn't allow that to happen and she probably asked her father, a retired FBI agent to help her get Jason out of the picture so she could continue to live a lavish life in a large mansion located inside of a gated community. It is unclear if Molly had any psychological issues at the time of the slaying, but she was diagnosed with bipolar depression in the past which could explain her erratic behavior that cost this innocent man his life.

Early life

Molly Corbett was born as Molly Martens in 1984 to an all-American family from Tennessee that always took great care of each other. Her father was an FBI agent who worked very hard to make his family have a comfortable life. He had a really good relationship with his children and made his best to be in their lives as much as possible. As a matter of fact, Thomas Martens and his wife Sharon had four children – three boys and one girl. Molly went to a high school in Tennessee and was a solid student. She wasn't at the top of her class, but her grades were good. Therefore, when the time to continue her education came, she was accepted to Carolina College.

Even though her parents weren't incredibly rich, they did have enough money to buy Molly her own place. So she lived alone in her apartment during the college years. Molly was incredibly good-looking, and it comes as no surprise to find out that she started modeling at one point. She didn't have a nationwide success, but she did earn enough money to start living on her own. She had an incredible physique thanks to years and years of vigorous training. Molly particularly enjoyed swimming and worked as a coach for a short period of time. Once she was out of college, Molly started a relationship with a man living in Ohio. The two of them became engaged, and Molly was very comfortable with him.

She confided to him that she was diagnosed with bipolar depression as a teenager and that she struggled to keep it under control. However, Molly wasn't ashamed of her diagnosis and actively sought help from the professionals. She was prescribed antidepressants and attended therapy regularly which helped her function normally on a daily basis. Molly started spending the majority of her time between North Carolina where her parents lived and Ohio. But it seemed like she wasn't particularly happy with the situation because her decision to leave the restaurant where she was working for years shocked everyone who knew her.

In a complete turn of the events, Molly found an advertisement posted by a wealthy Irish businessman who needed a nanny or an au pair. Without any hesitation, Molly contacted him, and that was the beginning of a whole new life chapter for her. She was ready to start over in another country, and this was a perfect chance for her.

Meeting Jason Corbett

Jason Corbett lived in Limerick, Ireland his entire life. He was a successful businessman who married in his late twenties to his long-time girlfriend whom he loved very much. They got two little children – Jack and Sarah in a very short period of time. However, tragedy struck this young family when Jason's wife died after the complications of an asthma attack. This left Jason all alone with two youngsters who needed attention and care. Unable to provide them with constant supervision because he needed to work, Jason made a decision to hire an au pair who would look after the children and run his household. After all, he was a successful businessman who was often on the road, taking business trips all around the country. Molly Martens applied for the job and Jason hired her right away. She seemed very responsible, and Jason also liked that she was quite beautiful.

Very excited about traveling abroad and seeing Ireland, Molly left the United States quickly, without informing anyone, including her then fiance. Molly did a great job taking care of the children and Jason started enjoying her company more and more. After all, he spent all of his free time with Molly and his young ones. On the other hand, Molly loved the fact that she was living in a very large luxury home which was an upgrade for her. After just a couple of months with the Corbetts, Molly, and Jason started their relationship. They got engaged in 2011 and made a decision to get married on June 4th the same year. Jason craved a stable family life and saw an ideal partner in Molly. After all, the children adored her, and she was very responsible.

Molly wanted the fairytale wedding and she persuaded Jason to go to Tennessee for the ceremony. Even though it meant that all of his family needed to travel overseas in order to attend, he wanted to please his future wife. The wedding was supposed to take place at the Bleak House which is a very famous mansion in Tennessee with a long history. Molly was walked down the aisle by her father, and Jason's children were a part of the ceremony. The wedding itself was beautiful, and all the guests thought that Jason was finally happy. After all, he deserved it after losing the love of his life, and the relatives were sure that Molly would be an ideal step-mother to Jack and Sarah.

The newlyweds returned to Limerick, Ireland after the ceremony but Molly really missed the United States and her family. She asked Jason to move to the States which was a complicated process because his company was stationed in Ireland. Jason wanted to make things work with Molly, so he managed to relocate his business to Lexington, North Carolina. He bought a luxury property for his family in Davidson County, and it seemed like everything was great for the Corbetts. But Jason gradually started to miss his old life and family back in Ireland. He was constantly homesick and didn't feel very comfortable in the United States.

Another problem was the adoption of Jack and Sarah. Molly insisted that they make her their legal step-mother. However, Jason was against it for some reason, and that increased the tensions between the two of them. Molly insisted to have the equal rights to the children and Jason constantly refused. On the other hand, Molly loved the fact that her family was only a couple of hours drive away from her and they visited each other often.

The night of the murder

On the night of August 2nd, 2015, Karen Black Capps, the dispatcher received a frightening call. It was made by Thomas Martens, a retired FBI agent who asked for assistance in his daughter's home because he bludgeoned her husband in the head while trying to save his daughter from him. The 911 dispatcher stayed as calm as possible, guiding both Molly and Thomas how to give the man a CPR over the phone. However, the dispatcher noticed that both of them were very calm and almost emotionless. She was used to frantic 911 calls where a person on the other side of the line is doing everything they could to save an injured individual. Molly did inform the dispatcher that she was familiar with CPR but that she is too shaken to perform it at the moment. Even though people do have different reactions in situations like these, Molly's wording did seem odd to the dispatcher, and it remained in her memory.

When the paramedics arrived at a luxurious Panther Creek home of Jason Corbett, they were shocked by the look of the crime scene – the blood was everywhere, and his corpse was almost unrecognizable. He was brutally bludgeoned in the head with a baseball bat, just like his father-in-law said. But they did notice another strange detail, and that was the fact that Jason's body was cold to the touch, suggesting that Molly and Thomas didn't contact the emergency services right away and that they possibly waited for some time to seek assistance. This suggested that they probably wanted to make sure Jason is dead and that no one can save him. The police were called to the scene as well because they needed to take statements from all the parties who were involved in the attack which was a standard procedure.

Molly's story was that the children woke up in the middle of the night because one of them had a nightmare and they cried or screamed. She wasn't sure, but Molly was on her feet immediately. Molly went to their room right away to calm them down and put Jack and Sarah back to bed. It took her a couple of minutes, but the children were sound asleep afterward. After that, she went back to the bedroom she shared with Jason. According to Molly, Jason was agitated she woke him up in the middle of the night, and he jumped on top of her. He did work long hours, and it seemed like he was under a lot of pressure lately. Jason put his hands around Molly's neck and started choking her. At first, she was startled and unable to defend herself because he was never violent towards her. However, she managed to scream when Jason's grip loosened a little bit. Molly said that this was the moment that probably saved her life. Luckily, her father Thomas Martens was staying with them at the time because he was visiting and he was sleeping in the basement bedroom reserved for guests. Thomas heard the screams and ran up the stairs, unsure what he would find.

He was a trained FBI agent and sensed that something sinister was going on. After seeing his daughter being choked, Thomas quickly grabbed a baseball bat and started hitting Jason in the head in order to make him let go of her. Thomas would later say: *"I don't know what precisely woke me up, but what I heard were loud voices and thumping like something bad was going on. So I grabbed that baseball bat and I ran upstairs."* Molly added more information to this story by saying: *"He wanted to shut me up so he covered my mouth and he started choking me. But at some point when he stopped, I screamed. The next thing I remember is my dad standing in the doorway."*

Considering their statements, the police did think that the general story checked out. However, a further investigation was needed, especially because the crime scene was particularly brutal and there were a couple of details that stood out right away, such as the fact that Jason had his bags packed and there were children clothes inside as well. Jason's family was devastated when they heard the news of his passing, and they immediately said that the police should take a closer look at Molly because their marriage was not going well lately. As a matter of fact, according to Jason's sister Tracey Corbett-Lynch, Jason was planning to leave Molly and the United States that same week. He already set everything up for his move back to Limerick, Ireland. Tracey told the police that Molly was probably not happy with Jason's decision to move away and possibly divorce her so she did everything she could to keep the luxurious house for herself and that included the murder.

The autopsy and aftermath

Jason's lifeless body was sent to the coroner because the cause of death needed to be confirmed. The investigators were told that Thomas used a baseball bat in order to save his daughter from her husband, but that statement needed to be supported by the evidence. The coroner was absolutely shocked when he saw Jason Corbett's body. His head was completely bashed in, and the wounds seemed too brutal. The coroner would later say that he saw similar wounds on car crash victims. In the end, the coroner was unable to say for certain how many times Jason was hit in the face. However, some wounds were inconsistent and they appeared to be made by a different weapon. The police did uncover a landscaping stone in the house, and it stood out to them. It was picked up as possible evidence, and they were very right. Some wounds were made with this brick, and neither Molly or Thomas mentioned it. There was an indication that he was also hit after his death, suggesting that this was a clear case of a rage killing.

The toxicology report uncovered even more inconsistencies. Jason Corbett had a large dosage of sleeping pills in his system which gave the impression that he was passed out as the attack happened. He didn't have a prescription for them, but Molly did. As a matter of fact, she picked up a brand new bottle that same week. It is not uncommon for people to share medications, especially if someone needs to sleep and they can't for some reason. However, the number of sleeping pills found in Jason would certainly knock him out if he never used them before. Also, the lack of defense injuries suggests that Jason was unconscious. After all, if he was attacking Molly and she was trying to get him off of her, there would certainly be at least a couple of scratches. The medical examiner concluded that Jason Corbett was probably brutally killed by his wife Molly and her father Thomas.

Meanwhile, Molly continued to fight for the custody of Jason's children. However, both Jack and Sarah were sent back to Ireland to Tracey and David Lynch. Having in mind that Tracey was Jason's sister, it comes as no surprise that the children were given to her. The investigation progressed rapidly, and Molly and her father Thomas were arrested in January of 2015. The detectives had enough evidence to suspect they have planned and executed a murder. Not to forget that they tried to cover it up by staging the string of the events that apparently led to the manslaughter.

The trial

The trial for the murder of Jason Corbett started in the middle of July 2017 in North Carolina where the crime itself happened. Both Molly Corbett and her father Thomas Martens pleaded self-defense and the defense of the other which was a clever move from their team of lawyers. However, the prosecution had enough time to build a solid case against Molly Corbett and her father Thomas. They analyzed the findings by the medical examiner and talked to many witnesses who knew both Molly and Jason. Jason's family was the most knowledgeable which was expected since they talked on the phone with each other often.

Jason's sister Tracy provided a clear insight into what was going on with the Corbetts at the time of the murder. She said the following: *"His heart never really left Limerick. He formed some really good friendships in America but always missed Limerick. He was a real Limerick man – loved the rugby, loved the golf."* Tracy also implied that the main reason for the murder was the fact that Jason planned to go back home to Ireland and take the children with him. Molly was quite attached to them, and she couldn't cope with the possible loss. Plus, the fact that Jason refused to officially allow her to adopt his children was devastating to Molly. She practically raised them and was with Jack and Sarah from their early childhood.

The prosecution dug even deeper because the attorneys do know that there could be a financial gain behind every killing. Assistant district attorney Greg Brown revealed that Jason Corbett had a life insurance policy to his name and that Molly would be paid a total of $600,000 in case of Jason's death. Tracy also testified on the stand that Molly was eager to leave her brother Jason, but the only thing stopping her was the fact that she would not see his children ever again. According to Tracy, she was contacted by a friend of Molly's who claimed that she confessed to them that she reconciled with her ex-boyfriend and planned to find a way to get Jason out of the picture as soon as possible.

Tracy Lynch's testimony was the lengthiest one during the trial, but that was assumed because she had plenty of information about her brother and his marriage. After all, she got to know Molly over the years. However, Tracy didn't have anything positive to say about Molly except for the fact that she took good care of Jason's children. Tracy revealed to the courtroom that Molly was a liar who made up the stories such as that she had numerous miscarriages, and that was the reason why she cannot have children of her own. Plus, Tracy said that she witnessed Molly being abusive to Jack, Jason's little boy. Jason's sister also added that Molly adored Sarah and that she forced the girl to call her mom. Apparently, it was incredibly important to Molly to be addressed in this way. She would blackmail the children if they refused to call her mom. Molly stood up for herself in the court, saying that those were lies.

However, the most defying moment of the trial was the showing of the crime scene photos. Assistant District Attorney Alan Martin first started to describe the room where the murder happened, signalizing around the courtroom in order to present the jury with accurate information about the blood spatter which was another detail that proved how brutal the attack was. Once the photos were shown to the jury, one of them became physically sick and needed to get out of the courtroom. The images showed badly beaten Jason Corbett with an unrecognizable face.

The prosecution repeated the medical examiner's findings of the murder weapons, confirming that Jason was beaten with both a baseball bat and a brick. Although the investigators cannot say for sure, it is possible that Thomas Martens used the bat while Molly Corbett hit Jason with a brick. Their defense teams tried to justify the violence shown by saying that Molly and her father were afraid that Jason might actually kill them, so the fact they used too much force was somehow alright. After all, they were trying to defend themselves because according to their version of the story, Jason was the aggressor. The prosecution then added that neither Thomas or Molly had any kind of injuries which was odd for someone who was attacked.

One of the last witnesses to appear on the stand was Karen Black Capps. She was the 911 dispatcher who received Thomas Martens' call on the night of the murder. She remembered that neither Thomas or Molly sounded like they were trying to save Jason Corbett. Instead, she had a feeling that they were putting on the show for the authorities, knowing that the call will be recorded. David Freedman and Walter Holton who were in the defense team objected to these claims, saying that Capps' opinion is irrelevant for the case and that she is not a proper witness. The judge accepted the objection, saying it was Capps' observation, not the facts. However, the prosecution did get a chance to play the 911 call in the courtroom, allowing the jury to hear it for themselves.

The closing statements included a dramatic monologue by the prosecution that described the possible last seconds of Jason's life. The defense relied their case on the fact that Thomas Martens was an FBI agent which spoke volumes about his integrity and professionalism. As a matter of fact, David Freedman who was one of his lawyers said the following: *"Who is more likely to have snapped that night - a 65 year old grandfather who has protected us in his life from terrorists and drug dealers or a man, from his own mouth, feeling dizziness when not taking their medication."*

Thomas Martens confirmed the self-defense claims by saying: *"I did not murder my son-in-law. And I would challenge any reasonable man, much less a reasonable father, to say that this was unnecessary force. I used the force that was necessary to end the threat. That's what I was trained to do for over 31 years, end the deadly threat."* The trial lasted for a bit more than three weeks and the jury didn't liberate for too long. On August 9th, 2017 they found Molly Corbett and Thomas

Martens guilty of second-degree murder. Both of them received twenty to twenty-five-year sentence.

Life in prison

The news about Molly Corbett didn't stop once she was behind the bars. She made the headlines once again when the house she shared with Jason in Panther Creek was finally sold. The house itself stood empty for years since there were no buyers. But the new tenants moved in July of 2018, and they paid plenty of money for the property because it is a part of a gated community. Molly is set to receive $172,000 since she was also the owner of the house. The other half of the money will go to Sarah and Jack Corbett. It is very likely that Molly Corbett will not see the money at all because she needs to pay her defense team. Her legal bills are also pretty high.

In August of 2018, several media outlets reported that Molly Corbett broke the prison rules and that her sentence has been increased for four years. Jason's family was quite vocal about this because they were not satisfied with the fact that she didn't get life in prison as it was expected. They shared their approval all over the social media, praising the North Carolina law that forced Molly to be transferred back to a high-security facility.

More news about Molly and her life behind the bars got to the media in September of 2018. The public was shocked to learn that Molly had a new job in North Carolina Correctional Institute of Women where she is currently staying. The prisoners who get accepted into this program are required to work in a call center connected with the Board of Tourism of North Carolina. They are supposed to inform the callers about the events, things to see, where to stay, etc. There is also a chance of a reduced sentence which is probably appealing to Molly Corbett. The fact that she got accepted into this program can reduce Molly's sentence by four to five years.

Molly Corbett and Thomas Martens also filed an appeal to the sentencing the same month. Their lawyers said that they are basing the appeal on jury misconduct. Apparently, the jury talked among themselves outside of the courtroom, sharing the information and opinions about Molly Corbett. This had a huge impact on the trial itself because the jury didn't follow the evidence presented by the defense, meaning that the private conversations had an impact on the final decision. The defense lawyers also claimed that the judge refused to give the permission to present the evidence that Jason was actually a violent person who might have harmed his first wife. The final decision will be made in a couple of months, and then Molly Corbett and Thomas Martens will know if their sentence will be reduced or if they will be granted a new trial.

MYRA HINDLEY

DEAN STEPHENS

22

In the early 1960s, Myra Hindley took her first job out of school at a small chemical company called Millwards Merchandise. A shy eighteen-year-old, she kept to herself, reading in the office courtyard during breaks.

But she only did this to attract her co-worker, Ian Brady.

Brady would spend his breaks reading books. Myra soon followed suit in the hopes that he would approach.

After several months, the Glasgow, Scotland native finally made his move.

They both worked at the office as clerks. Brady was four years older than her as they began to date.

Myra lived with her grandmother and gave her virginity to the awkward co-worker on her grandmother's sofa. She would soon become Brady's accomplice in some of the most gruesome child killings in the history of Great Britain.

A BAD NEWS CHARACTER

Brady already had a police record for petty theft. He also had a strange demeanor, tilting his head oddly at people as he stared them down with hooded eyes.

He was nicknamed "Lassie", not a reference to the Collie dog but to his feminine body language. Brady was tall, skinny and would indicate later that he was a bisexual. As a child, he had few friends and was called "Dracula" in the neighborhood. He would torture kittens and see how long it took for them to die.

They were both bookworms and Brady would give Myra books on the Marquis De Sade, trying to introduce her to the world of sexual sadism. After their dates, he would invite her back to his place and play back recordings of Adolph Hitler's speeches.

The young couple would come up with pet nicknames for each other. Myra would call Ian "Hetty" after a character in the Goons and he would call her "Hess" after Hitler's deputy. They would soon become inseparable, both strangely odd people that felt that were superior and set apart from everyone else.

It soon became clear, however, that Ian was influencing Myra and not the other way around. He was her guide to the world of sexual sadism and then later, slowly revealed his desire to rape and murder children.

He started this by sharing a book in the same way he introduced her to sadomasochism. The book had detailed the "crime of the century". A child was the victim and one of the characters was named Myra.

"He had given me a book called 'Compulsion'," Myra recalled. "Which was the story of Leopold and Loeb. They decided to commit the perfect murder. They were studying the philosophy of Nietzsche, his theory of the superiority of the pure Aryan and the strong overcoming the weak. It was very much the Nazi philosophy. They kidnapped a twelve-year-old boy for a ransom. They killed him, were caught and sent to prison. I told him it was a very disturbing book. But why exactly had he wanted me to read it? He told me he wanted to do a perfect murder and I was going to help him. That was why he needed me to pick someone up as I was a woman and a child would be more trusting of a woman. I burst into tears and he slapped my head backward and forward. I managed to fight him off and told him to stop it."

Myra fell prey to Ian's system of push and pull psychology. He would be abusive to Myra then inexplicably turn around and be sweet to her.

"I must be totally honest and say he wasn't always cruel and sadistic towards me," Myra said. "We had some pleasant times in country places that he'd found during his travels on his bike. We'd pack a picnic lunch, lots of coffee, bottles of wine and spend whole days in peace and tranquility. That was such a contrast to the other side of him. These were moments I treasured and thought about when things were bad. Trying to remember, telling myself that he couldn't help what he was and maybe in time he would become accustomed to ordinary domesticity and we could live a normal life."

IDLE HANDS

"Myra was a bored English girl looking for some adventure," forensic psychologist Paula Orange said. "Brady had an edge about him. Myra liked that about him, she wanted out of her dull life and into a world of edgy darkness, if you will."

Myra didn't judge Brady for being an avowed Nazi. She thought he was just going through a phase but he continued to play Richard Wagner's music full blast and storm around the house dressed up in Nazi regalia. Working himself up into a frenzy, he would then play rough sex games with Myra.

Myra found this aspect of Brady's personality to be alluring. She enjoyed dressing up in leather and black stockings, indulging whatever fantasy Brady could come up with.

"She was a sheltered young woman," Orange said. "And Brady opened up a whole new world to her. Think of it as 'Fifty Shades of Grey' with some Nazism thrown in and you have the whole relationship of Myra Hindley and Ian Brady."

The kinky sex continued and Brady gave stronger indications that he wanted to commit the perfect murder.

He wanted to harm children.

But he needed an accomplice.

"We can make the case that Myra made the jump from sadomasochistic sex to murder out of an obligation to Ian," Orange said. "It gave her a rush, to follow his lead. She needed more and more to get that same high."

The two would feed off each other sexually after which Ian would begin to plot the murders out. Who would be their victim? How would they kill them? Where would they kill them? He wrote things out in advance to the most minute detail.

"She (Myra) became desperate to fulfill his fantasies, his needs," journalist Clint Entwhistle said. "She was frightened, I suspect, of rejection by him."

So Myra didn't report him. She went along with his program.

SNAPPED

Brady had made his decision that they were going to kill someone. The night before, he took Myra to a bar on the back of his motorcycle. The two parked a little beyond the pub itself. Ian then began to intimidate Myra. He was jealous that she took a ride home from a co-worker.

"All the time we were talking," Myra recalled. "He was running a knife across his fingers. I honestly thought he was going to stab me. Then he laughed, put the knife away, told me never to accept a lift (the co-worker) again, and we drove back to the pub."

"Later as we were driving home, I dreaded what he would do when we got there, for I knew he would do something. "He raped me anally, urinated inside me and, whilst doing so, began strangling me until I nearly passed out. Then he bit me on the cheekbone, just below my right eye, until my face began to bleed. I tried to fight him off strangling me and biting me, but the more I did, the more the pressure increased. Before he left, when he'd seen the state of my face, he told me to stay off work the next day ..."

This would all take place under the roof of Myra's grandmother who was asleep when the assault took place.

"My gran almost fainted when she saw me and went to get my mother, who asked me if 'He' had done that to me. My mother disliked him intensely and kept telling me he was no good for me; she'd been telling me that since I'd met him at 18 and a half, but what girl of that age listens to her mother when she is wholly infatuated and in love? I told them what he had told me to say (she had been hit by a beer bottle during a bar fight) but I knew they didn't believe me."

THE FIRST MURDER

The following night after he beat down Myra, Brady selected his first victim.

He spotted a teenage girl walking to a dance by herself. She wore a sky blue jacket over a button-down red polka dot dress. Her white gloves and high heels turned on Ian Brady but what really arrested his attention was her face.

Cute with an air of innocence. A face that had an easy vulnerability, someone who would crack under the pressure of his whip.

Her pain and tears would be delicious, Ian thought.

Her name was Pauline Reede.

Brady gave Ian her orders and told her to pick the girl up. He would follow them on his bike.

"Ian Brady was awkward," Entwistle said. "He was not the kind of person a child would trust. There is no way anyone would have gotten into a car with him."

That is what he needed Myra for.

Myra did as he said, driving up alongside Pauline as she walked on the deserted road. The two young woman had already known each other from around the neighborhood.

"Can I give you a lift?" Myra asked.

"Oh, thank you, sure," Polly got into the small white van.

"Where are you going?"

"To the dance hall-"

"Okay," Myra said. "I just have to go to the Moors. I just lost one of my gloves. You can help me look for it. It will only take a second."

Pauline simply nodded her head. She trusted Myra.

THE KILLING FIELDS

"The Moors above Manchester were a special place for Ian Brady and Myra Hindley," Entwistle said. "They picnicked there together. They'd have sex there. It was a very, very important place to them."

It would also be the place where they would commit their first murder together.

Myra stepped off the van and directed Polly to look through some bushes. It was dark and Pauline asked if they should just look for it in the morning. Myra laughed it off and walked away, feigning as if she were looking for her gloves.

Ian Brady waited in the bushes, his mouth dry with anticipation, as he watched the sixteen-year-old Polly sift through the bushes.

Sneaking behind his victim, he slammed her across the head with a shovel.

Pauline Reede fell to the ground, stunned.

She would then be raped, tortured then murdered by the sadistic Brady.

"Brady was a sadist," Orange said. "He got off on the suffering of his young victim. The more innocent she was, the more she screamed, the more she pleaded for her life, the more he got off. It was part of the high for him. He had moved beyond the bedroom thrills with Myra and needed a bigger high. He wanted his fantasy to become reality."

Brady assaulted Pauline until she lost consciousness.

No longer able to provide him the "fun" of listening to her suffer, he took a knife to her throat and killed her.

Myra watched in silence as Ian Brady commit the brutal crime and then proceeded to bury Polly in a shallow grave.

"He led me to her body which I tried not to look at," Myra wrote. "I didn't know at the time that he was testing me at there was no need for me to be there. He told me to look at here. I'll never be able to forget what I saw. I stood and looked at the dark outline of the rocks against the horizon of the dark sky. Three people died that night. Pauline. My soul. And God. No God would have let what had happened, happen."

On the surface, however, Myra didn't seem distressed about the murder. She went to work the following Monday as if nothing happened.

"You would think if she had any conscience left she would have gone to the authorities," Orange said. "But Myra had been dehumanized by that point. The daily rapes and assaults made her numb to everything."

Still, a part of her old self remained. The disappearance of Pauline Reade sent shockwaves throughout Manchester. Myra was reading the newspaper one day and noticed a personal column written by Pauline Reade's mother.

It read " Pauline, please come home. We're heartbroken for you."

"I began to cry," Myra recalled. "Rocking myself back and forth with the paper clutched to my chest. I didn't hear his bike, nor knew that he'd come into the house. He asked me what was wrong but I couldn't answer; I couldn't stop shaking and crying, for I was devastated about what had happened to Pauline, and for her mum and dad. I really liked Mrs. Reade and used to feel sorry for her because she had problems with her nerves and always looked as though she was on the edge of a breakdown. He grabbed the paper off me and soon saw what I'd seen."

"He put the bolt on the front door in case gran came back, did the same to the back door, and began to strangle me. Before I lost consciousness, I heard him remind me of what he'd said after Pauline's murder, and that threat still stood. After the first murder, as we were driving home, he told me that if I'd shown any signs of backing out, I would have finished up in the same grave as Pauline."

MYRA'S EARLY LIFE

As one would expect, Myra grew up in an abusive home.

Her parents engaged in daily shouting matches which she watched from behind her bedroom door.

Her father would routinely beat her mother, exposing Myra to sudden violence during her formative years. He was a competitive boxer who would also engage in weekend bar brawls.

"He used to beat her a lot," Entwhistle said. "Her father was a very, very powerful influence on her life. She had a tough personality type to start with. If you combine that with a violent childhood, a childhood where she was taught how to be violent, how to be aggressive, then you end up with an unusual personality type."

Myra hated her father and saw him as a bully. He would teach her to box, often hitting her across the head when she performed the techniques incorrectly.

"My father wielded total parental control," Myra said. "I rebelled against it. Fought against it. All my life until I was old enough to free myself from it. All his attempts to control me, even the successful ones were at great cost and were the result of bitter recriminations and often a hard physical punishment."

Myra's father would give her spankings without warning, leaving her buttocks bruised.

Once when she was bullied by a little boy and came home with bruises on her face, her father locked her out of the house. He told her to either face down the bully or he was going to beat her up himself.

"I set up the street to meet my persecutor," Myra recalled. "I quickly concentrated on whatDad had told me and showed me. As Kenny's hand came up, I shot up my left hand, fist bunched towards his head. As I predicted, both hands went up to protect his face and I lifted my right hand and slammed it into his tummy, hitting him hard. With a gasp, Kenny Holden's knees crumbled and before he could recover I slammed my left fist into the side of his head. Kenny was so heavily shocked he sat down heavily on the floor and burst into tears. I stood looking down at him triumphantly."

Myra saw a lot of her father in Ian Brady. Aggressive. Ultra-violent.

"Myra did what we call in psychology, 'transference,'" Orange said. "She saw in Ian what she saw in her father. She never got her daddy's love. So in her mind, she saw Ian as Daddy. She wanted Daddy's love and would do whatever Ian wanted. That was part of her cycle. Transferring a deep need for her father's love onto Ian. There is the strong possibility that had Myra never hooked up with Ian she would have never become a murderer. But the two of them together? Horrific results."

"The bringing together of Myra Hindley and Ian Brady," Entwhistle said. "Unleashed an appalling set of criminal acts."

POLLY IS STILL MISSING

The disappearance of Polly Reede sent the town of Manchester on edge. Things like that simply didn't happen there.

"The fact that children were being abducted and killed," Entwhistle said. "Was incomprehensible to the ordinary man and woman in the street."

Myra would soon find out that Ian's sexual fantasies were not limited to teenaged girls.

He wanted boys too.

Myra would again be a willing accomplice in procuring Ian's second victim. This time, it would be twelve-year-old John Killbride. Myra would befriend the young boy before bringing him to the Moors where he would be sexually assaulted by Brady and later killed.

"I had a terrible feeling something had happened to him," John Killbridge's mother recalled when her son didn't come home from school. "Because he wasn't the kind of boy who would leave home for any reason. He was quite happy and very pleasant, always singing and whistling and I just couldn't see him going anywhere with anyone. Unless it was in an innocent way, somebody wanting to do a job with him or something like that. He'd be enticed into a car that way."

Ian would take photos of the body and burial site. This would become part of their ritual, their ceremony. They would perform the murder then take photographs as if to mark the moment. Then they would return to the scene of the crime days after with their dog "Puppet" in tow. They would take more pictures and relive what took place only days earlier.

"He stopped me as I was walking (to take a picture)," Myra recalled. "And said to turnaround. Moved me about a bit. Told me to kneel down and look at 'Puppet' whose head was showing when he was still wrapped inside my coat. I now know, and knew quite soon afterward, that he photographed me virtually kneeling on John Killbride's grave."

AN INSATIABLE HUNGER

Four months had elapsed between the Pauline and John Killbride murders. But now Ian could not wait long. He ordered Myra to deliver another victim to the isolated Moors.

His name was Keith Bennett. An exuberant, trusting boy, Keith looked like the proverbial nerd with a gap-toothed smile and professorial eyeglasses.

"Keith was a cheeky little lad," Entwhistle said. "He liked to go out and have fun."

Trusting that Myra was taking him some place fun, the young Keith was ambushed by Brady who wrapped a cord around his neck.

Myra did her usual best to remain detached while the horrific attack took place.

"I hadn't wanted this to happen," Myra recalled. "I was tense and terrified. I tried to concentrate my mind miles away from where I was. Finally, after roughly what I think was a half an hour by which time dusk began to descend. I heard him whistle or call. When I stood up, he was waving me back down to the stream bed. Virtually nothing was said as we made our way back except for him saying the spade was hampering him and he'd have to hide it, which he did."

The twelve-year-old Keith, whose entire family was waiting for him at his grandmother's house, never showed up.

His entire family would be traumatized for life.

"I am a mother," Keith's mother, Winnie Johnson said. "It was my first lad and I've got to find him no matter what."

Keith Bennett's body was never found.

"I have nightmares," Johnson said. "I jump in my sleep. It's getting to me now. Because I just can't get him back."

Meanwhile, Myra and Ian would once again take mementos of their time together, taking photos of themselves along the Moors on Keith's fresh grave. Days later, the two would go to St. James Church for midnight mass.

"I retained a warm religious glow," Myra said. "And came out feeling warmed. Not so Ian who took a long swill of whiskey and went to the grave where he casually urinated."

RITUALS

The photos of their time together became an obsession for Ian Brady. He had an automatic camera where he would set the timer and pose for photographs with Myra. In a few of them, they would pose on top of the fresh graves with Ian playfully choking Myra.

"Myra and Ian would often return to the scenes of their crimes," Orange said. "They would take photos of themselves there and relive the thrill of committing the murders."

Over time, however, the photos would not be enough stimulation. They needed something better. Something more visceral.

Sounds.

Ian Brady decided he would record the audio of their next victim being tortured.

That next victim would be ten-year-old Leslie Ann Downey. Myra would befriend and abduct her from the county fairgrounds.

"They would take her back to their home," Entwistle said. "Where he photographed her and recorded her being tortured."

Ian Brady would listen to the audio tape over and over again, closing his eyes and remembering the horrific acts he committed.

Is is the murder of Leslie that Myra would refuse to talk about in interviews.

"There's a tape that isn't what people think it is," Myra said, trying to downplay her own sadism evident in the tapes. "But it's bad. I just hurt so much to think that I've been such a cruel bastard."

THE RUSH OF KILLING

Like a drug addict needing a bigger hit to get high, Brady needed more and more of a thrill for his next murder. He started to get sloppy whereas before his attacks were meticulously planned out.

His next victim would be Edward Evans.

"Edwards was sixteen, seventeen years old," Entwhistle said. "And he picked him up in a pub in Manchester."

This would be the first time Ian acted in tandem with Myra to obtain the victim. They enticed the young man to come over to their home and there were witnesses in the pub.

The couple also invited Myra's brother in law, Dave Smith to watch the carnage.

"Smith had no idea what was going on," Entwhistle said. "He walked into it totally cold, totally unaware and soon found out that he was involved in the most horrific scene with blood all over the place. A man's head being smashed in."

Smith was appalled, then called the police and told them of the killing.

Police arrived on scene within minutes. They discovered the mauled body of Edwards in a tub. Both Ian and Myra would be arrested.

"It is inexplicable as to why the couple would allow Dave Smith to witness the murder," Orange said. "A part of me thinks that it was part of increasing the thrill. The desire to share what they felt was a special moment with someone else."

A CHILLING DISCOVERY

Investigators would then scour the home, finding one unusual clue that would reveal the goings on of the couple now known in the papers as the Moors Murderers.

They found a left over luggage ticket.

The police would go to the central train station and matched the ticket with a suitcase. Inside, the found something they would never forget.

"They kept trophies in suitcases," Entwhistle said. "In there, of course, was the tape recording of Leslie Ann Downey and that proved what they'd done."

The police would play back the tapes. It churned their stomach to hear the tearful cries of Leslie Ann Downey plead for her life.

"You need to do what he says," Hindley screamed at the little girl. "I told you to shut your face!"

"I want to go home," the little girl pleaded.

"Quiet! Do you not speak English?"

The tape would be played for the jurors at the trial of the couple.

According to witnesses, you could hear a pin drop when they played the tape in court.

"Afterward there was a long, stony silence," Entwhistle said. "As people reflected on what they just heard."

DENIAL

Myra would maintain her own innocence of the murders and repeatedly state that she never witnessed any of the killings herself.

"My solicitor (defense attorney) told me they'd found the body of a child," Myra said. "Identified as Lesley Ann Downey, did I know anything about it? And I said 'No.' A week after that, I'm not sure, they found John Killbride's body and they charged me with, I think it was the murder of John Killbride. Yes, it was. They set me down behind a table and behind it was a large poster of John Killbride. 'Will you just identify these pictures or these photos and tell us if you seen them before.' I'd say, yes, and then they turned over the picture to another photo of the unearthed body of John Killbride."

The picture, Myra would state, made her cry.

LETTERS TO MOMMA

Myra would write her mother numerous letters before her trial. She would order her mother to destroy the letters after she read them but her mother thought otherwise. She would also tell her mother to keep the photographs of her and Ian to herself.

"Don't believe what they're saying about us," Myra wrote. "It is all lies."

But the mothers of all the victims didn't see it that way.

In court, they all had an opportunity to confront Myra.

"The worst part was being confronted by Mrs. West in the witness box," Myra recalled. "And I was looking at her as she was giving evidence and she saw me looking at her and she screamed across at me. 'How can you look at me?' And she called me every name under the sun."

It is at this point that Myra stated that she began to fully realize the gravity of her crimes.

"It suddenly hit me just what I'd done and I think he (Ian) sensed this," Myra said. "We were sitting next to each other and he just put his hand on my arm and squeezed my arm. And I turned around and looked at him, and he was telling me with his eyes to keep quiet."

The jury would find them guilty and in May of 1966 both would be sentenced to life in prison.

STANDING BY HER MAN

Myra refused to testify against Ian. There were some legal experts at the time who believed that if she gave evidence against Brady she would have walked free. But she didn't. She elected to take the punishment along with him.

Instead, she accepted her sentencing and continued to write her mother.

"Dear Mum," Myra wrote. "I knew that I would have to go to prison for some time for 'harboring'. But I didn't think it would be for this long. Ian is in prison, in the special wing. Poor thing, he sews mailbags during the day. He says it helps to pass the time quicker than expected. Will you do one thing for me, ma'am? Take out a policy on me or for me, for a half gram a week. I can't even begin to think of the future. It will be something to fall back on."

"Ian has got a little mouse in his cell. He feeds it crumbs and sits in bed watching it nibble them. The other night, he left it half a chip, thinking it wouldn't touch it but when he woke up the next morning it had disappeared."

Over the next three years, Myra would bombard her mother with requests for the photographs of her and Ian together. She said she did this at the behest of Ian who wanted both the slides and photographs desperately. Myra's mother eventually relented by was sure to allow the police copies of the negatives.

"Ian wanted those pictures back so bad because it reminded him of the events," Orange said. "That is the sort of thing we've come to expect from certain types of serial killers. They want to relive the moment in their fantasy. They'll take mementos, pictures, different elements of their crime in order so they can relive it in their minds. The pictures of Myra holding their dog on those burial sites were of paramount importance to Ian."

Myra would die in prison in 2002 of respiratory failure. Her ashes would be scattered over the Moors, a place that she loved so much.

"Was Myra Hindley sick or was she evil?" Entwhistle asked. "She had a violent father. She met a sexually sadistic man who desperately wanted to be a serial killer. All those things came together and made her carry out some evil, appalling crimes."

Ian Brady remains alive, living out his years under suicide watch in a psychiatric facility where he has repeatedly stated that he will kill himself if given the chance.

MASTER MANIPULATOR : THE TRUE STORY OF SERIAL KILLER KIM SNIBSON

SUSAN GRAHAM

"Why is this happening?"

Those may have been Greg Hosa's last audible words as Andrew Flentjar and Stacy Lea-Caton brutally forced him to the ground. The answer Flentjar gave would shock not just Hosa, but both of his attackers. For it was that response that would have allowed both Flentjar and Lea-Caton to realize that they were not part of the just cause they had believed themselves to be, but were in fact at the mercy of Kim Snibson's deluded and volatile plan.

Kim Snibson is a master manipulator who was envious of the life Greg Hosa and his wife Kathryn McKay had built together. Most notably, their horse farm. Situated in Nowra, New South Wales, Champagne Shires would be considered a small property when compared to the amount of land horse farms usually covered. Still, despite its modest size, it was far grander that Snibson could ever hope to own herself. For her, Champagne Shires was the perfect combination of all her fondest desires and life passions. Living next door to her dream made reality, it didn't take long for her fantasies of owning the property to become a perceived right. Snibson's greed led her to believe that she deserved Champagne Shires, while her ego convinced her that she could have it, if only the current owners were dealt away with.

Once Hosa and McKay had agreed to stable her horse, Snibson had the perfect excuse to visit her neighbors. She would come by often and grew to know both Hosa and McKay well. This access only fuelled her lust for the property and her disdain for the happy owners. Unaware of Snibson's feelings towards them, Hosa and McKay remained kind and generous to their neighbor. On one known occasion, Snibson had fallen behind in payments and owed the couple $300 for the care of her horse. Hosa and McKay had agreed to continue to stable her horse and told Snibson that she could pay them when she was able. This generosity did not provoke gratitude in Snibson, but instead fed into her increasing resentment. By this time she had begun to believe that she could force the couple to sign over the rights to Champagne Shires to her, kill them, and live happily on the property without consequence. Rationally this plan is ludicrous, but given her past success, Snibson believed it to be perfect.

Years earlier Snibson had inherited her house in Calymea Street, Nowra Hill, from an elderly woman named Judith Plankas. It was this property that had made her a neighbor of Hosa and McKay, and ultimately, it was in this house that the couple would be murdered. But it wasn't until after her arrest that questions began to arise as to exactly why and how Ms Plankas came to deed the property to Snibson.

In an interview with Take-5 Magazine, Snibson's ex-husband recalled how Ms Snibson had befriended Ms Plankas. At the time, the elderly dog breeder had been diagnosed with cancer and had needed help taking care of her animals. Snibson had been quick to offer assistance and for a while must have struck the sickly Ms Plankas as a Godsend. But, as Mr Snibson told Take-5 Magazine, "Kim got hold of powerful tranquilizers and quietly killed the older dogs." Perhaps accustomed to Kim's crueler actions, or blinded by devotion, it is believed that Mr Snibson neglected to inform Plankas of what Kim had done. By all appearances, Ms Plankas had no idea what kind of woman she had welcomed into her home.

"Then on April 17, 2003," Mr Snibson recalled, "Judith's condition suddenly worsened. She changed her will that night, leaving the house to Kim, and died the next day."

This would not be the first time Mr Snibson had been privy to the threat Kim posed to those around her. And it would not be the only time his failure to believe or act lead to disastrous consequences. In the same interview, he revealed a conversation he had once had with a woman named Rebecca. She had only been 15-years-old when Ms Snibson had convinced her to move out of the home and in with the Snibson family.

"We've got a free babysitter," Ms Snibson had announced when she had brought the teenager home, according to her ex-husband. He went on to say that, "later, Rebecca sought me out and what she had to say rocked me. Kim had kept a horse at a stable owned by an elderly couple and Rebecca said (that Kim) talked about tying them up, making them sign over their property to her and killing them."

Still, it would seem that Mr Snibson was not then willing to believe his wife capable of such things. But Rebecca wasn't Snibson's first nor only attempt at recruiting accomplices in her murder plot. Nor was the teenager's confession the only one to be dismissed. Armed with vicious lies and a willingness to manipulate all those around her, Snibson approached numerous people. Perhaps it is a testament to her skill at manipulation, or her ability to choose those reluctant to cause a stir without any solid evidence, but many of the people she approached never spoke of the conversations until after she had been arrested. Mr Snibson claimed that was when he began to receive calls from dozens of friends, most of which started with 'I've been wanting to tell you this for years'.

"Then they'd tell me about an affair she'd had or how she'd tried to enlist them in a desperate scheme to have someone beaten up or killed," he told Take-5 Magazine. He also spoke about how a friend had told him that 'Kim had wanted an old lady beaten up because she said her son had molested one of your girls'. "Nobody has touched my daughters," Mr Snibson said. "It was a fantasy made up by Kim to get others to do terrible things for her."

With so many people aware of the true, malicious nature of Snibson, it is baffling how few people voiced their concerns to law enforcement. Snibson continued her search for willing participants until she found two men who believed her lies. Her first recruit was Andrew Flentjar. He was a neighbor of the Snibson family, although Mr Snibson insists that he didn't know Flentjar that well, and had believed that Snibson hadn't either.

"She didn't socialize with (him) or stay for a cuppa," he had said in an interview. But still Snibson had managed to make the otherwise reasonable man willing to help her in her plan to kidnap and assault Mr Hosa.

"Andrew was told by Kim that the couple had sexually abused her child and had videoed the episode," Paul Leask, a Crown Prosecutor for New South Wales, reviled on the television show Deadly Women.

In her interview on the same television show, a journalist for Illawarra Mercury Newspaper, Veronica Apap, attested that there had been "no evidence at any time in court that Kathryn or Greg had engaged in anything like that." Still, Flintjar believed the story Snibson wove and, under the impression that her plan only involved minor assault as justice for her daughter, agreed to help.

Snibson then approached Stacy Lea-Caton, a former neighbor who had been in trouble with the law. Mr Snibson remembers Lea-Caton as being a man who continuously worked to create a notable reputation for himself as a dangerous man.

"You would be talking about normal things," Mr Snibson told Ms Apap during an interview, "and Stacey would come in with something bigger or better. He talked about his criminal history, stuff like that."

Mr Snibson went on to say that when it came to Mr Lea-Caton he "didn't believe anything he told me", and that, "I didn't think he would go very well in a fight, myself. He is not this tough person he was making himself out to be."

Ms Snibson, however, saw a potential for violence in Lea-Caton and knew just how to bring it to the surface. During a visit she tested the waters by telling him a lie similar to the one she had recruited Flintjar with. According to Leask, "Stacey Lea-Caton was told by her that the couple had drugged her, sexually assaulted her, and videoed the episode."

Once again there she could produce any evidence in support of her claims, nor could later investigators. According to Apap, "It seems to be a total fantasy on her part" and Mr Snibson has stated that "Greg Hosa was a thoroughly decent person who did not deserve such terrible lies to be made up about him, let alone die so needlessly." Still, Snibson was convincing enough to for Lea-Coton to push aside his desire to get his life back on track and he soon found himself alongside Flintjar, embroiled in Snibson's supposed plan for vigilante justice.

"She employed a means of modulating the story depending on the person who was the recipient of it. To press the right buttons." Leask asserted. "The theme was always one of sexual impropriety and of course, nothing excites people's sympathy more than that."

With her two accomplices waiting for instructions, Snibson put her plan into action on January 28th, 2006. It was easy to lure Hosa to her home. The 56-year-old man didn't suspect that anything might be wrong when Snibson called and asked him to come over.

"He came quickly after that conversation occurred," Apap said in her Deadly Women interview. "He didn't think that he was in any danger or that there would be any problem."

Lea-Carton and Flintjar swarmed Hosa as he entered the Snibson home. Using a slab of wood they struck him on the head and forced him to the ground. The men then proceeded to hogtie Hosa, forcing him onto his stomach and binding his legs to his hands. It was during this attack that Hosa asked his assailants "why is this happening?" While the exact wording cannot be determined, it is reported that Flintjar responded by accusing Hosa of pedophilia.

With this declaration both of Snibson's henchmen realized that they had been lied to. They were blindsided by the revelation yet, having participated in assault and kidnapping, and still unaware of just how malicious Snibson's intentions were, neither felt they were in a position to leave. Snibson deceit had taken them past the point of no return and both were at a loss at what to do next. This afforded Snibson the perfect environment to maintain control.

While the men watched over a struggling Hosa, Snibson called his wife and 'confessed' that she and Hosa had been having an affair. It was a story that few would believe and later would be seen by their family as adding a foul insult to considerable injury. Jan Keily, a sister of McKay, would attest that they family was 'disgusted' by the claim. But on that night, it was enough to draw McKay into Snibon's trap.

Just like her husband, 44-year-old McKay was set upon by Lea-Carton and Flintjar. She too was hogtied and gagged by having a sock forced into her mouth and taped into place. Once again the men found themselves forced into a situation far from what they had been expecting when Snibson left to retrieve two 44-gallon drums from Champagne Shires and brought them to the house.

After shoving Ms McKay into one of the drums Snibson disclosed the needlessly cruel method she had chosen in order to kill McKay. "She murdered Kathryn by wrapping tape around her face and eyes and nose," Leask described.

Many factors must be considered when determining how long it would take an individual to suffocate to death. First, oxygen deprivation renders the victim unconscious. If they are still unable to breath brain damage will begin. As a general guide, it is believed to take approximately 5-6 minutes for death to occur. Snibson, Lea-Carton, and Flintjar stood by and watched McKay struggle for this entire length of time. When arrested, all three would give varying statements as to what exactly had happened that night, but in all versions, the two men who had not agreed to murder still made no attempt to save Ms McKay.

When Snibson turned her attention back to Hosa, she had a different method in mind for his execution. According to Leask, "Kim killed Greg Hosa by garrotting him with electrical wire. Kim killed them both deliberately and methodically." And once again, her now reluctant accomplices failed to put an end to her actions.

As night fell the trio loaded the two barrels, each now filled with the corpses of a once loving couple, into the back of Snibson's truck. Together the three drove to a remote patch of the Tomerong State Forest. Here she doused the remains of Ms McKay and Mr Hosa with petrol and set them alight.

As Leask stated, "Incinerating the bodies was done for no other purpose than to destroy evidence that those two poor people had ever been to Kim's house that day."

For all her obsession and manipulation, it took only hours for Snibson's plan to come undone. As it would turn out, Mr Snibson's reading of Stacey Lea-Caton's character had been far more reliable that Kim's had been. The only known criminal within the trio, Lea-Carton was unable to suppress his guilty conscious and within hours of leaving Snibson confessed to his sister and her husband. The series of events he told them had been highly edited but it was still damning enough that the young couple had insisted that he tell the authorities. At 2:30am they had taken him to the Nowra Police Station to report the crime. According to police, Lea-Caton had originally stated that he had seen a man and woman tried up at the farm and was worried that they might come to harm. By 8:00am they had arrested Snibson. A whole day hadn't passed by the time police located the remains of Greg Hosa and Kathryn McKay. Superintendent Kyle Stewart would describe the discovery as a "horrific scene", while Leask provided greater detail. "All that remained of Kathryn was her right foot and little remained of Greg."

But even when caught Snibson was far from willing to admit to her actions. In her statements to the police, she was a hapless witness to a domestic disturbance that spiraled out of control. According to Snibson, she had informed Ms McKay that she had been having an affair with Mr Hosa. Hosa had come to her home first, followed by and enraged Ms McKay. Once there, the couple had begun to argue. The confrontation soon grew volatile and in the heat of the moment Lea-Caton had picked up a bird perch and struck Mr Hose over the head hard enough that he fell to the ground. She recounted how this hadn't deterred Ms McKay who had then turned her anger onto Snibson herself. McKay had become so furious that she had 'come at' Snibson. This had forced Flentjar, who had also happened to be present, to tackle the older woman to keep her from harming Snibson.

"She fell back and hit her head on the pantry and fell on the floor," Snibson told police. She further went on to explain that is was after Ms McKay had been injured that Lea-Caton's murderous intent rose to the surface. In

Snibson's version of events, it was Lea-Caton that strangled Hosa with a rope before forcing her to wrap tape around McKay's head until, as she insisted he had instructed, 'she turned blue'. In his final act of depravity, Lea-Caton had been the one to light the bodies on fire.

Her behavior at the trials of her accomplices was a far cry from what others had observed during her own trial. While giving evidence in the New South Wales Supreme Court, Snibson broke down into tears as she described the "gurgling sounds" Mr Hosa made as the life was choked out of him. Snibson would tell the court that she felt "sick to my stomach" about the murders. She continued to say that she thought about it "every single day." She had become so unsettled that Justice Terence Buddin had to adjourn the sentencing hearing for five minutes to give her time to compose herself.

Compared to her behavior and demeanor at other times it was almost possible to believe Ms Snibson was two entirely different people. For Leask, there was no doubt which persona was ligament and which she put on for self-preservation.

"There will be no remorse from Kim Snibson. It's not in her nature," he had said in an interview. He also claimed that Snibson is a person "that lacks the quality that makes us human beings." But perhaps his opinion on Snibson was most elegantly and directly described within his statement, "I have been involved in some shocking crimes involving some dreadful brutality. This case stands out because, in my career,

I can only reasonably expect to come across one or two sociopaths. And that's what Kim Snibson is."

It is a sentiment echoed by Candice DeLong, a former criminal profiler for the Federal Bureau of Investigation who often lends her insights to programs such as Deadly Women. "It's unlikely Kim feels remorse for what she did. Sociopaths never do," she said during an interview. She further asserted that "if she ever does emerge from prison, watch out."

It is DeLong's opinion that "Kim is a natural born killer. She wanted to commit murder," but for those like her ex-husband, Snibson is not so clearly an evil woman. While he called her 'pure evil' in an interview with Take-5 Magazine it was also discovered that he had withheld information from investigators in a bid to protect her from prosecution.

"I did tell the truth in all statements," he told the New South Wales Supreme Court. "I left out those couple of sentences from Kim because it sounded very damning to me. I didn't want to see anything bad happen to her. I still had loyalty to Kim even though we had long broken up."

Some of these omitted sentences referred to statements Ms Snibson had made the day after her arrest. According to Mr Snibson, she had said "Don't worry about me, I'm a bad person", and had alluded that she would be 'going away' for 30 years. He further stated that Snibson had said that while she did want to tell him what had happened on the night of the murders her lawyer had instructed her not to talk about it. "She said when she gets to court and has her say, the truth will come out."

Whether Mr Snibson truly believes in his ex-wife's innocence or not, he unwittingly brought more evidence against her. When Detective Sergeant Jason Hogan had asked Mr Snibson to take them to where he as Ms Snibson used to train their dogs for dog sled competitions he had agreed. The location he had led them to had been the where the smoldering barrels holding the remains of McKay and Hosa had been found. In the same day, he had also unknowingly brought the police to the part of Braidwood Road where Mr Hosa's burnt out four-wheel drive had been discovered.

Andrew Wayne Flentjar was the first to be sentenced. He is currently serving a minimum of 10-years for his role in assisting in the kidnapping of Hosa and McKay. Stacey Lea-Caton pleaded guilty to aiding and abetting murder and received a sentence of a minimum 16 years, with the maximum time served of 22-years.

Lea-Caton testified against Snibson during her trail and put a great amount of pressure on her supposed version of events. Combined with the sight of the 44-gallon drums, similar to those used to dispose of McKay and Hosa's remains, which were brought into the courtroom, the cracks in Snibson's account of that night were beginning to show. Whatever the 10 men and 2 women of the jury had truly believed was rendered moot when, approximately halfway through her trial, Snibson changed her plea to guilty.

On September 5th, 2008 Snibson faced her sentencing hearing. By Australian law, those affected by a crime have the right to lodge and read out a victim impact statement to the court and the perpetrator. The friends and family of Hosa and McKay took advantage of this opportunity. Marion, Katheryn McKay's sister, described how the murders had rendered her family into a state similar to 'animals caught in headlights'. In her statement, she explained how she struggled "to find the words for the numbness and traumatic feelings the murders caused the family."

Marion described the impact of their loss and Snibson's actions as being felt "physically, socially, emotionally and psychologically." How her family is no longer able to watch programs about horses or the news, as they stir up too many painful memories. How her work as a counselor has suffered and that the majority of her grief-stricken family has since abandoned their homes in Nowra.

She described McKay and Hosa as loving, community-minded people, and reminded the court and Snibson that her sister had been a nurse with a natural drive and desire to help other people. She reiterated how their senseless and brutal deaths have had a lasting impact on hundreds of other people and how more than 500 people had attended their funerals. Somewhere within this speech, Kim Snibson reportedly began to cry.

Another of McKay's sisters, Jan Keily, spoke of her utter confusion at how Snibson, Flintjar, and Lea-Caton could have brought themselves to do what they had done. She also addressed how insulting it was to the memories or their loved ones that Snibson still maintained that there had been an affair, not to mention the accusations she had made about McKay's intended violence towards Snibson. "The families are shocked by the lies that have been told about Kathryn McKay and Gregory Hosa by the three offenders."

Justice Buddin commended the sisters for the dignity and grace they had shown while delivering their statements before adjourning the proceedings. When he delivered the final verdict, Justice Buddin gave his own opinion on the case before him. He expressed how the crimes against this kind-hearted couple had been committed with a "considerable degree of callousness".

Justice Buddin explored the suffering that was inflicted upon Mr Hosa and Ms McKay, not just at the agonizingly slow and painful death, but at the mental torture that must have endured at the hands of the captors. He expressed how they were forced to wait for a "not inconsiderable amount of time", stuck in a state of anguish, wondering what their kidnappers would decide to do to them. "They were totally defenseless and at the mercy of the offenders," he said.

Justice Buddin then turned his attention to the version of events that Snibson had put forth, the version of events that left her as a victim of circumstances and Lea-Coton's vicious nature. He described this story as "implausible", "quite fanciful" and "tailored to suit inescapable, objective facts". As proof of the ridiculousness of her claims, he pointed to her recruitment of accomplices. This was not an act of a woman caught off guard by a lover's spat but instead was indicative of the level of calculation and manipulation she was capable of wilfully wielding.

While Snibson had told the court that she was sorry for the role she had played in the couple's grizzly end, Justice Buddin was not swayed. He explained that he had not believed her words to be those of someone truly remorseful and repentant, but instead said that whatever contrition she had expressed struck him as contrived. His final verdict had been a jail sentence of no less than 32 years. This means that Snibson would be 60-years-old before she becomes eligible to apply for parole.

The town of Nowra is still healing from the horrors of that singular night. As Paul Leask has stated, "that one of their own was the killer was something that psychologically traumatized that community." The senseless cruelty Snibson brought down upon a devoted, generous couple has only been magnified by the ridiculousness of her plan. For all the action she was willing to take there was no way her plan would allow her to gain ownership of Champagne Shire, rendering her depraved actions useless and her goal unattainable.

But perhaps what is hardest for the residents of Nowra, and all that hear of the tragic deaths of McKay and Hosa, to come to terms with, is the wealth of opportunities presented for people to intervene. Be it out of embarrassment or social delicacy, those who had concerns over Sibson's actions had refused to disclose what they had known. At the time it might have been dismissed as a personal eccentricity, a misunderstanding, or a benign threat, but now blaze as warning signs for the brutality that was to come. Perhaps if those who had felt the inkling of concern had stepped forward a different course could have been plotted and McKay and Hosa could have been spared. But then it is also possible that nothing could have deterred Snibson, and that these murders were the only end her insatiable greed would have allowed. Wherever the truth may lie, it is too late to act for McKay and Hosa. Their lives have already been sacrificed on the altar of Snibson's pride. The only solace that is to be garnished now is that Snibson has been removed from the general population and will hopefully be unable to claim any further victims. But what little comfort this offers will forever be overshadowed by the influence Snibon's name will forever provoke. Those who learn about the merciless crimes this woman visited upon the people who would have been her friends will undoubtedly no longer be able to look at their neighbors without there being the lingering question of 'what if?'

BURY THEM ALIVE : THE TRUE STORY OF SERIAL KILLER TIFFANY COLE

JESSICA WINSTON

When James "Reggie" and Carol Sumner moved to Jacksonville, Florida for their retirement, they had visions of good health and happiness. They never thought that their overnight invitation to long-time South Carolina neighbor, Tiffany Cole, would end up the way it did; With the Sumner couple being buried alive.

Reggie and Carol Sumner were high school sweethearts in North Charleston, South Carolina. They were the kind of couple that everyone envied as they walked down the hall. Unfortunately, their lives pulled them in different directions. Reggie decided to serve his country in the navy. After finishing his tour, he got married and landed a job with the railroad. Carol also married and became a devoted mother, however, her first marriage ended in divorce, and her second nearly killed her. In 1987, after years of abuse, her husband at the time shot her seven times in their home before driving away and turning the gun on himself. Her daughter, Rhonda Alford, just ten years old at that time, spent almost a year helping her mother recover from her wounds. She had to help her bathe, dress, and take care of the house. After taking eight years to fully recover, Carol went back to work as soon as she was able. For over twenty-five years she was a civil servant at the Citadel and the Charleston Air Force Base. She also worked a second job at night at a Belk department store, among other jobs she would take when needed. She did whatever she had to in order to make ends meet. Shortly after her recovery, she found out that the blood transfusion she had received during her previous trauma had given her Hepatitis C. She was angry because she felt as though she could not escape her late ex-husband, but she refused to let it ruin her life. She soon started a new job at a cable company and it was during this time that her life finally changed for the better. Nearly forty years after they'd left high school, a chance encounter brought Carol and Reggie together again. One night in 2000, a phone call was made to the cable company where Carol was working, which she received. After talking with the customer Carol and learning his name, she realized that he also sounded just like the Reggie she remembered. So she asked him if he was the same Reggie Sumner who attended Garrett High school in South Charleston. It was. They decided that they should get together after not seeing each other in so long. This time, though they were inseparable. Like "teenagers in love", a quick courtship led to love and then marriage in 2001 with a ceremony at Carol's home in West Ashley. Carol's daughter has said of Reggie "he was just a very gentle, kind and giving spirit. You could not ask for a better friend, husband or stepfather." Eventually, after retiring, the couple decided to move from South Carolina to Jacksonville, Florida. Reggie had previously bought a house during his days working for CSX railroad and as he was a "brittle" diabetic in frail health, he thought he would be more comfortable in the warmer climate. Carol agreed. "She only went down there to honor her husband," Rhonda said. Before moving, they decided to sell their Chevrolet Lumina to the stepdaughter of a friend who lived down the street, Tiffany Cole. They allowed her to make payments on the car to help her out and she agreed, often driving down to Jacksonville with friends to make those payments. Tiffany and the Sumners became friends and Tiffany would often spend the night at their house when she and her friends went down south. A pleasant girl on the outside, the Sumners had no idea what Tiffany could really be like.

Tiffany Ann Cole was born on December 3, 1981, to her sixteen-year-old mother, Shirley Duncan. Her biological father was in jail. She had no male role model to look up to or who could offer her protection the way a father should. Her mother had a boyfriend, but he was beyond cruel and especially loved to torment Tiffany. At one point, she had a puppy which her stepdad threw against a wall, breaking its neck right in front of her. He was abusive verbally as well as physically and Tiffany claims that as a young girl, he began to molest her, beginning around age eight. As a young teenager, she turned to alcohol and drugs to deal with the pain. In high school, Tiffany was a student who participated in cheerleading and played the flute. She was also a girl scout member but eventually the alcohol and drugs took over her life and she quit her programs and dropped out of school. At one point she fell in love with a boy with severe epilepsy, who ended up breaking her heart and since the only example of love from a man came from an abusive stepfather, this breakup reinforced the belief that she should expect to be treated badly and let down by men. She began looking for love in all the wrong places. In May of 2005, during a six-month period of prostitution, Tiffany ran into a man by the name of Michael Jackson. They were drawn to each other right away and began to get high and sleep together.

Michael James Jackson, born May 12, 1982, had a significant criminal history beginning in childhood. Born to a drug-addicted mother, he was mostly raised by his grandmother. He had multiple felony convictions but only for things like fraud and theft. After meeting Tiffany and becoming close, they took a road trip, first going to Myrtle Beach, then driving to Jacksonville, Florida, where they would be staying with Michael's best friend, Alan Wade. Born May 22, 1987, Alan and Michael had known each other for just over a year. When Tiffany and Michael arrived in Florida, they stayed at Alan's mom's house. After just a few days, though, she kicked them out because she was tired of the loud noises and constant partying. With nowhere else to go and with all their money spent on the nights of drinking and partying, Tiffany remembered that the Sumners lived nearby. The three friends showed up at their doorstep and explained what had happened. The couple was very happy to see Tiffany and invited her and her friends to stay the night. While they were chatting and catching up, Carol mentioned how worried they had been about their house in North Carolina not selling. There was no need to worry, however, because not only did their property sell, but they had also made a $99,000 profit. It was this general statement to a long-time neighbor that sealed the Sumner's fate.

It's difficult to know just whose idea it was to rob the Sumner's. Some say it was both Tiffany and Michael, while others say it was Michael who was the plan maker and master manipulator. Either way, a plan was hatched to rob and kill the loving couple. At some point in June, Alan had contacted his friend, Bruce Nixon Jr., and told him of a plan to rob someone. No other details were given. Then on July 6th, Alan called Bruce, born May 9th, 1987, and asked him if he would be interested in joining the others in digging a hole. Bruce agreed and stole four shovels from his neighborhood. The other three friends drove to Bruce's house in a rented Mazda RX-8 that Tiffany had rented in South Carolina. The group drove around hoping to find a perfectly remote place for the hole to be dug. Alan asked Bruce if he knew of any good places to which Bruce responded that he did. He took them into Georgia, to a wooded area just over the state line. Leaving the car parked on the road, the group walked through the wooded area into a clearing where they began to dig a hole while Tiffany held a flashlight. It was approximately four feet deep and six feet square. Upon completion of the hole, they left the shovels and went back to the car. It was here that Alan asked Michael if Bruce could join in on their robbery plan. Michael agreed. The foursome drove back to Alan's house but his mother would not allow Michael in as she believed him to be a bad influence on her son. Over the next couple of days, it was

Tiffany's job to remain in contact with Carol and Reggie in order to gain information from them about their plans and whereabouts. The foursome also secretly watched the house in order to figure out the Sumner's routine. It was unclear yet as to whether or not the group would enter the home while the couple was gone or if they would simply go in with the couple there. It was ultimately decided that they would enter the home while the couple was there so that they could get their financial information and the means to access their accounts. Michael said that he would kill the victims by injecting them with a lethal dose of their medications. He then promised that the four friends would split the money they received from the Sumner's accounts, each receiving about $50,000. They began making preparations for their plan. Just after midnight on July 8th, 2005, Michael, Tiffany, and Alan went to Wal-Mart and purchased disposable rubber gloves. On the evening of the murders, they went to an Office Depot, where Tiffany bought duct tape and a large roll of plastic wrap. Last, they bought a toy gun that shot plastic pellets.

Around 10pm., on July 8th, 2005, Tiffany drove the other three group members to the Sumner's house in the Mazda. Herself and Michael remained in the car while Alan and Bruce went up to the door. They had the duct tape and toy gun and both were wearing the plastic gloves. After Carol answered the door, Bruce and Alan told her that they were having car trouble and asked if they could use their phone. Carol said of course they could and invited them in. As soon as the boys entered the home, Alan pulled the phone cord out of the wall. Bruce pointed the gun at the couple. Alan grabbed Reggie around the neck and pushed him down into a chair. They told the couple that they wanted credit and debit cards and any other financial information. Carol began pleading with the boys not to hurt them. Bruce took the couple into a spare bedroom where he used duct tape to bind their legs and hands and to cover their mouths and eyes. Alan sent a text message to Michael, informing him that everything was under control. Michael then also entered the home and he and Alan began searching for financial information. They saw a pile of mail and financial statements which they put into a plastic bag. They spotted Reggie's prized coin collection and took that too. Michael told the other two to take the couple into the garage at which point they put them into the trunk of the Lincoln Town car. Tiffany went into the house and grabbed some of their belongings, put them into a bag and took the bag with her to the Mazda. Following the plan, both cars headed towards the gravesite, stopping only once to put gas in the Lincoln. Upon arrival at the site, Michael opened the trunk and apparently began screaming when he saw that the duct tape had become loose and the couple had worked the tape off. It had been over 100 degrees in the trunk. Sweat had caused the tape to loosen. They had also taken the tape off their eyes and were huddled together. Michael ordered Bruce to tape them up again, which he did. Alan then attempted to back up the car to the edge of the grave but, unable to do so, Bruce took over. Michael then sent Bruce up the road to wait with Tiffany at the Mazda. While still alive, the Sumners were taken out of the trunk and pushed into the hole. It is unclear as to who actually did the burying because Alan and Michael each blamed the other. Somehow, Michael ended up getting the personal identification number of the Sumner's bank account. Reports differ on whether he obtained this information from somewhere in the house or if Carol told him the number while being threatened to be buried alive. According to one documentary, Carol had gotten the tape off her mouth again when in the hole. Michael was telling them that if they didn't give up their PIN, they would die, at which point Carol yelled it out. It didn't seem to matter either way though because they continued to shovel dirt onto the scared couple.

After filling the hole, Alan and Michael put the shovels back into the trunk of the Lincoln and drove it up the road to where Tiffany and Bruce were waiting with the Mazda. The four of them drove to

Sanderson, Florida, where they abandoned the Lincoln after wiping it clean of fingerprints. They then drove back to Jacksonville where they immediately went to an ATM and withdrew money from the Sumner's account, before retiring to a hotel. Alan and Tiffany went to another Wal-Mart where they purchased more latex gloves as well as bleach. They returned to the Sumner's home in order to clean up any evidence. They also stole a computer. Bruce stayed with the group for another day and then went home, but Alan remained with Michael and Tiffany who returned to South Carolina, where Tiffany rented two hotel rooms; one for herself and Michael and one for Alan. It should be noted that after returning home, Bruce went to a party with a plastic bag filled with different medications. At one point he announced that he had found a new job murdering people. He stated that he had buried people alive and killed them without mentioning the involvement of anyone else.

On the morning of July 10th, Carol's daughter, Rhonda, decided to report to police the fact that she hadn't been able to get hold of her mother for a few days. Since they kept in touch on a regular basis and spoke every couple days, it was highly unusual for her mother to not return her calls. The next day, the Jacksonville Sheriff's Office (JSO) went to the Sumner's home. The back door of the house was unlocked and in the kitchen there dirty after-dinner plates, which was also highly unusual for the couple. The JSO began to investigate the financial accounts of the couple and they found that large amounts of money had been withdrawn within a short time frame. Video footage from the ATM machines that the group had used showed Michael's face and the silver Mazda in the background. On July 12th, after Rhonda made a plea on local TV networks for the safe return of her parents, the Sheriff's office received a phone call from someone posing as Reggie Sumner. Dispatch contacted Detective David Meacham of the Sheriff's office and put the caller through.

Meacham: Where are you at?

Michael: We're in Delaware right now

Meacham: And what city is that in?

Michael: It's in Corpus

Meacham: Corpus, Delaware?

Michael: Yes

However, the town of Corpus, Delaware does not exist. Next, Tiffany came on the phone posing as Carol.

Meacham: Is this Carol?

Tiffany: Yes, sir, it is.

Meacham: Okay. This is Detective Meacham from the Sheriff's office. How are you doing tonight?

Tiffany: I was sleeping

Meacham: I understand. I understand you have some health problems

Tiffany: Mmhmm

Meacham: Okay. Any other problems?

Tiffany: I'm really tired right now

Meacham: What kind of problems do you have?

Tiffany: Cancer

Meacham: Cancer?

Tiffany: Mmhmm

The detective called Rhonda into the station so that she could listen to the taped conversation. She confirmed that the people posing as the Sumners were definitely not Carol and Reggie. The main reason for the call was to ensure everyone that the Sumners were alive and well and because the bank accounts had been frozen. They asked the detectives to reinstate the accounts, which they did so that they could track the money in order to locate the perpetrators. They also had the phone number from which Michael had called. Using this information, they were able to find that the phone was registered to Michael and that a call had been placed to a car rental agency in Charleston. They also learned that the cell had been used near the Sumner's home the night of the murders. Detective Meacham contacted the rental company and was told that the car had been rented to a Tiffany Cole and that it was overdue. Using the rental car's GPS system, they were able to find that the car had also been near the Sumner's residence during the time of the abduction. Using the cell phone trace, the car's GPS and the photos of Michael at different ATMs, police were able to locate the general whereabouts of the three murderers. On July 14th, with help from Tiffany's brother, who was on probation and threatened with jail, police raided a Best Western hotel in Charleston and arrested Tiffany Cole, Alan Wade, and Michael Jackson. Bruce Nixon was also picked up at his home in Florida.

While Tiffany, Michael, and Alan refused to cooperate with law enforcement, Bruce appeared to have some semblance of a conscience because he broke down and admitted to the crimes right away. He also agreed to lead police to the burial site. For the first time in TV history, documentary footage showed Bruce and detectives at the grave site where Bruce broke down in sobs. Excavation of the site began the next day. The victims were found fully clothed in a crouching position. Reggie had somehow broken his tape and was holding Carol's hand. There was two feet of dirt over their heads. With ten years of homicide under his belt, Detective Meacham said it was one of the saddest and most horrible things he had ever seen. The medical examiner determined that both Reggie and Carol were alive in the hole before they were buried. Their nostrils, mouths, throats, esophagi, and trachea had fine sprays of dirt in them, which indicated that they had inhaled it. They died from mechanical asphyxiation and smothering, caused by the dirt covering their heads while compressing their chests. She said it was the worst case of asphyxiation she'd ever seen. It was "horrendous."

At some point while in jail, but unaware that Bruce had come clean, Michael's grandmother called him.

Grandma: Michael, listen to me and don't say a word. You're in the newspaper. All over the newspaper yesterday and today

Michael: For what?

Grandma: Murder

Michael: What?!

Grandma: Murder. 'Bodies ID'd as former South Carolina couple James and Carol Sumner. Bail was denied for 18-year-old Bruce Nixon of Florida who was arrested and charged with murder, home invasion, robbery, and kidnapping.' He took them to the grave site and everything

Michael: Oh my God. Are you kidding me?

Grandma: It's right here in today's paper

Michael: Bruce took them to the f*****g spot. The f****r showed them where the spot was at?

Grandma: Yes, dear

Michael: *starts panting* Bruce just killed us all

Bruce Nixon told detectives everything that had happened and agreed to testify on behalf of the prosecution. He wasn't sentenced until after he testified against the other three group members, but in the end, he received 45 years for each victim, currently being served concurrently at Century Correctional Institution in Florida. Alan Wade was tried first.

Michael Jackson was the first to be tried. Testifying on his own behalf, Michael stated that the plan was only to rob the Sumners and that it was not going to involve murder. He said that Alan and Bruce went into the house and when they came out they drove off in the Lincoln which he then followed. He claims he had no idea that Reggie and Carol were in the trunk. According to Michael, when they arrived at the hole in Georgia, it was Alan and Bruce who told him where to park and to bring them a flashlight. It was when he arrived at the burial site that he heard Carol moan. He then stated that he questioned what the other two were doing before returning to the Mazda to wait. He did admit to impersonating Reggie. Bruce testified that Michael had been the ringleader and was the one who orchestrated everything.

After stepping down from the witness stand, Carol's daughter, Rhonda, said of Bruce, "I just wanted to hug him. He is a murderer, but in the end, he did the right thing." It was that testimony that she believed sealed Michael's fate because he was found guilty of first degree murder, robbery, and kid-napping, and sentenced to death for each murder. He is currently on death row in Florida.

Alan was next to be tried. Two witnesses who were not identified gave victim impact statements during the penalty phase. Alan's lawyer then called six of their own witnesses to testify including Bruce Nixon, Alan's mom and sister, the mother of a friend, his middle school principal, and his youth pastor. Overall, the witnesses testified that Alan's parents divorced when he was eight and his father disappeared from his life. His mother took him to church regularly and as a kid, he was kind, smart, and well-behaved. After the divorce, his mother was unable to spend a lot of time with him because she had to work a lot to support them. When he was in his teens, his mother had a bout with breast cancer. By his early teens, he began to use drugs. In the sixth grade, he was involuntarily committed to a 72-hour hold because of a drug related incident. When he was sixteen, his mom had to take him out of school or be arrested for his truancy. The next year, his mother kicked him out of the house in an attempt at tough love because his drug use was becoming worse. In 2004 Alan introduced her to Michael, whom she immediately saw as a bad influence on him. Since his arrest and before his trial, Alan had apparently become a model prisoner, obtained his G.E.D and tutored other inmates in math. Nothing seemed to sway the jury, however, because he was found guilty on all counts and voted eleven-to-one to receive the death penalty. He is also currently on death row in Florida.

Tiffany was the last to be tried. Her lawyer argued that she wasn't a major participant in the crimes. He said that she was under the control of her boyfriend Michael, and that he was the mastermind. Tiffany claimed that she believed the crime would only constitute a simple theft and that she didn't knowingly participate in the robberies, kidnapping or murders. She insisted that she did not know that Reggie and Carol were in the trunk of the Lincoln until they arrived at the burial site. The circuit judge, Michael Weatherby did not see it that way, stating that it was she who held the flashlight during the digging of the grave and was there when they were bound and placed in the trunk. He also noted that she was the one who purchased the duct tape and gloves and later pawned the jewelry and computer they had stolen. "She was thoroughly involved," Weatherby stated. "She knew exactly what she was doing and participated without hesitation." It was noted as well that she was the only one of the four who had previously known the Sumners. During the penalty phase, the prosecution called two of the victim's family members who gave impact statements. The defense attorney then called up witnesses who testified that Tiffany was of good character. Three of those witnesses were correctional officers who stated that Tiffany had been no trouble in jail and did not cause any problems. A psychiatrist, Dr. Earnest Miller, testified that she suffered from poly-substance and alcohol abuse, chronic depression, and a personality disorder. He also stated that she had witnessed abuse to family members and had been sexually abused herself by her stepfather. On the other hand, he testified that Tiffany was competent and thus he could not support a plea of insanity. Finally, he stated that she knew right from wrong and had a high average IQ. In the end, Tiffany was also found guilty of all charges and sentenced to death by a 9-3 vote. Upon hearing her fate, she bowed her head and turned to her mother, mouthing the words "I love you". Her lawyer, Quentin Till, said she had been ready for the decision. He visited her in jail that week. "I told her to be strong," he said. "...I still see her being utilized and manipulated by Michael Jackson." Revis Sumner, Reggie's brother, said that Tiffany has since written to the family, asking for forgiveness. He says he has forgiven her, but that doesn't mean she shouldn't suffer for her actions. The Reverend Jean Clark, Reggie's sister has said, "I pray for Tiffany.

I pray for all of them. I'm grieved that these four young people have wasted their lives." Chief Assistant State Attorney, Jay Plotkin, who tried all four cases said, "All of these defendants got exactly what they deserved. Justice was done." After the sentences were given and the trials were over, Reggie's son, Frederick Hallock, said, "You expect some sort of closure or some sort of good feeling when the verdict is read, but it didn't seem to help much. I just know they didn't deserve this." Currently, Tiffany is one of only five women on Florida's death row. At the time of her sentence, she was the sole woman there.

Tiffany, Michael, and Alan all filed appeals after their trials, citing multiple issues. All three were denied and their sentences were upheld. Recently, in 2015, Tiffany filed another appeal, asking for a new trial. She claims that her defense lawyers were ineffective and that she should not have been convicted of first-degree murder since she did not actually bury the bodies herself. But according to Florida law, it doesn't matter who actually committed the murder. Just knowing that it was going to happen is enough to warrant a guilty verdict. At her original trial Tiffany said, "But please remember I didn't do this. I am not the monster that created this, but I regret meeting him," referring to Michael. Upon hearing that Tiffany was asking for a new trial, Reggie's sister, Jean had this to say: "Most people are going to try to come back with something like that after the fact, because they're going to try to find a loophole and get off. But justice has a voice, and justice has to be served." And the thought of going through another trial breaks her heart. "I have family members that are still not the same and never will be the same. In fact, I don't like to involve them too much into things like this, because they can't deal with it."

In 2014, Alan Wade also filed an appeal for a new trial, citing that his lawyers did not do a good job of representing him. His appellate lawyers said that his original defense lawyers barely met with him before the trial and didn't interview witnesses prior to putting them on the stand. They also cited the lack of objections to supposedly questionable evidence. In December 2014, it was decided by the Supreme Court of Florida that his conviction be upheld.

Previous to that, Michael Jackson filed an appeal for a new trial, stating that his lawyers were also ineffective. As with Alan's trial, Michael claims that his lawyers did not make objections to certain evidence when there was clearly an objection to be made. The judge did allow an appeal hearing for his concerns and at the close of the hearing, Michael was allowed to make a statement. It went as follows:

First, I'd like to say that I am guilty of the crimes of first-degree murder, kidnapping, and robbery against Mr. and Mrs. Sumner. My reason for wanting to address the Court today is because of the many lies I told to everyone years ago at pretrial and then trial. I downplayed my involvement to look as if I were not guilty but the truth is that—the truth is that it was my idea to do this. Truly, I did not make anyone do anything. All were willing participants but I was, in fact, the leader. It was my idea to do it. I lied to this Court all throughout my trial testimony, same to [defense counsel and the State]. Even more so I lied to the people who deserve the truth the most, the family of Mr. and Mrs. Sumner, and for that, I am deeply sorry. There are no words that I could ever offer that would convey the depth of my remorse or sorrow, but again I say that I am truly sorry for what I have done and though I'm undeserving, I do ask forgiveness. My desire today is to reconcile the truth to the family of Mr. and Mrs. Sumner and to Your Honor, the attorneys and to the Court record. If necessary, I will answer any and all questions fully and truthfully. Thank you.

His conviction was upheld. Tiffany, Michael, Alan, and Bruce remain in jail today, with the former three on death row.

"It's sad," said Rhonda Alford about her parents. "It took them so long to find each other." Carol and Reggie's ashes sit in an urn in Rhonda's home, forever mixed and blended together.

THE BONDAGE MURDERS : THE TRUE STORY OF SHIRLEY WITHERS

MARY MAXWELL

Shirley Withers and Peter Shellard looked to be a mismatched couple.

Shellard was a multi-millionaire dollar real estate mogul and high-end car dealer. Logic would dictate that he would date much younger women, seducing aspiring actresses and models with his wealth. But Shirley was anything but a supermodel. She was an ordinary looking bookkeeper, thirty-three-years-old, and bit on the frumpy side.

"He was a hot shot," forensic psychologist Paula Orange said. "An eccentric hotshot but still very well-to-do. He would strut around town wearing fancy suits with matching socks but wear sandals over them. Shirley, on the other hand, was very unassuming. She looked like the typical cubicle drone. A little overweight and plain looking. Nothing sexy about her."

Their relationship, however, would be one of the biggest firestorms of sex, murder, and drugs in Australian history.

BEGINNINGS

Shirley was born in New Delhi, India in 1966. She immigrated with her family to Australia when she was a child. She married young and had two sons with her first husband. By 2000, she would be divorced and immediately be on the market for a new beau.

Enter Peter Shellard.

Peter, born in 1949, touted himself as a self-made millionaire although he had a benefactor in an older, maternal figure in Vera Moore.

He didn't finish high school, dropping out to obtain his real estate agent's license at night. Once he acquired that, he began leveraging properties around the Brighton area eventually making a fortune in addition to buying a high-end car dealership.

He called his company "Peter Shellard Real Estate" and then used that money to help finance a deal where he took control over Kellow-Falkiner Motors. He juggled both real estate as well as used Rolls-Royce and Bentley parts.

Shellard's businesses continued to flourish. He purchased many companies as well as commercial and rental properties.

"He hung around some heavy hitters in his area," Orange said. "People who could buy Rolls Royces without batting an eye."

Shellard would purchase the Rosecraddock Place in North Caulfield, a regal mansion which would later sell for over $7 million upon his death. As his wealth grew, he began collecting high-end cars which included a 1923 Rolls-Royce, a 1951 Rolls-Royce Silver Dawn, and a Mercedez-Benz 450SL convertible.

AN ECCENTRIC NUT

Shellard did have mental issues, however, suffering from bipolar disorder.

"His mansion was filled with all kinds of knick-knacks," Orange said. "Stuff that seemed disconnected and junky. But he was bipolar and people with that ailment tend to have different eccentricities. His was to hoard stuff among other things."

Shellard was reported to be a recluse, sheltering himself from the outside world as he became more wealthy. He had a barbed wire fence built high around the mansion but it served more to keep him in then keeping people out. His neighbors would rarely see him outside the compound unless he was walking his dogs. He also had ponies and kept an area for beehives. Neighbors complained about the bees and the city had the hives destroyed. Shellard would later file suit and demand that he have the remains of his dead bees returned.

Shellard would treat other homeowners as if they were peasants and would come and go on their private grounds as he pleased. One neighbor reported that Shellard came into their backyard and began sifting through their garden tools. Another complained that Shellard would park one of his Rolls-Royces in their personal garage. Shellard was informed to remove the vehicle after which he became enraged and began to tear apart the garage. He would then be sued for the action and was forced to pay almost $2000 in damages.

"Obviously, he walked around as if he had a sense of entitlement," Orange said. "Definitely a narcissistic sociopath but he could turn on the charm when he wanted. It all depended on what he wanted. When he was trying to make a sale, he could charm you. When he was doing something stupid and you called him on it, that is when he went berserk."

Town councilwoman Veronika Martens had plenty of bizarre dealings with Shellard as well. On one occasion, Shellard chopped down some cypress trees on his property and began burning the branches. Neighbors called to complain and firefighters came down to extinguish the flames.

Enraged, Shellard began attacking the firefighters and cut through the fire hoses with an ax.

Later, Shellard would be caught breaking into Caulfield Town Hall by climbing in through the roof. He would also come into the building unannounced, enter unoccupied offices and begin making phone calls.

"Shellard was an aggressive, anti-government guy," Orange said. "He went so far as to try to have his mansion designated as a religious place in order to avoid taxes. The judge got a good laugh at that one. The religion of what? Nutty behavior?"

Angered that his request was denied, he began making plans to tear down the mansion and divide up the land. But legal maneuverings blocked him from doing that as city council members had his mansion placed on the Historic Buildings Council, giving it legal protection.

A SADO-MASOCHIST

A ladies man, Shellard would marry twice. He had three daughters, Jenny, Clare and Sarah, before divorcing his second wife Elizabeth in 1994.

Shellard really did not have any bad habits that than his eccentricities as he abstained from both alcohol and smoking. He did have one fetish, however, and that was sadomasochism.

Shellard would go to clubs and participate in bondage sessions, preferring visits to the Hellfire Club in Brighton. Once there, he would "dress up in a full range of leather outfits and had belts with studs."

Shellard would go to the Hellfire Club to be whipped.

"He told me initially that his pain threshold was very low," Shellard's friend Christine Smith said. "And after a number of visits his tolerance for pain increased to the point where he really liked what was occurring. He found it very erotic."

By 2001, he was looking for a new partner and found one in Shirley Withers.

"Initially mum and I thought Shirley was a bit odd," Jenny, Shellard's eldest daughter recalled. "She would never look you in the eye. She was always very kind, though."

ENTER SHIRLEY WITHERS

Opposites attract, and Shellard soon began wooing Shirley with his luxurious lifestyle. He brought her numerous gifts, jewelry, and clothing.

"I'll bankroll all your dreams," he teased.

Shirley took him up on the offer, expressing her desire to run her own clothing boutique.

"Shellard did anything and everything for Shirley," forensic psychologist Paula Orange said. "He bought her everything she asked for evening financing her 'dream' of running a boutique store in a prestigious area of Brighton. Never mind the fact that Shirley had no business experience. Shellard believed he had money to burn."

"You can't be serious?" Shirley gushed when Peter told her he would buy her a clothing company.

"What are you going to call it?" Shellard asked, smiling.

"God," Shirley said. "God. I don't know. How about Suzette? Suzette Boutique?"

"Suzette Boutique!" Shellard laughed aloud as Shirley hugged him in appreciation.

Shellard made all the arrangements for Shirley to run the store. He had it designed and built to her specifications.

Shirley would have all of the brand name fashions in her store. She loaded the shelves with Marianna Hardwick, Charlie Brown, and Lisa Ho.

Shellard had one caveat and that was having his eldest daughter, Jenny, work in the boutique. Jenny herself, however, had a less than flattering impression of both Shirley and her attempts to run a business.

"My first impression when I started working there was that it was just a mess," Jenny said. "I couldn't understand how Shirley kept paying us every week. I had seen invoices totaling thousands of dollars and wondered where Shirley was getting the money. Shirley would just continuously buy stock for the business and for herself. She definitely had a problem with spending money."

Shellard did not stop at just buying Shirley her own boutique.

He bought her a house.

"It was a bit of an odd arrangement," Orange said. "They had separate living quarters. Shellard wanted his own house to himself and would visit Shirley for coital purposes."

Shellard displayed further bad judgment when he allowed Shirley to be put in charge of the accounting of his car dealership.

"He figured she was a bookkeeper," Orange said. "She must know what she's doing."

Shellard's naivete didn't end there as he allowed Shirley access to his property accounts in addition to becoming a signatory on his car dealership.

What Shellard didn't take into account was that Shirley was not a person he could trust nor did she know what she was doing.

Her boutique began to fail. She had purchased too much product and the few items that did sell would not have a high enough margin. Being a marginal business person, she continued to purchase inventory despite not generating any revenue.

The store began losing money. Lost of it.

So Shirley took it upon herself to begin stealing from Shellard's dealership. She would write checks to herself in upwards of $10,000. Shellard began noticing the discrepancies and called in his accountant.

After checking the books, the two realized that Shirley stole over $900,000, a significant amount of Shellard's wealth.

NO CURE FOR A SPENDAHOLIC

Shellard owned over eleven properties and his total net worth looked to be about $10-15 million.

By the time Shellard had finally got wind of Shirley's financial doings, she had amassed over $43,000 in credit card debt while her store was almost $275,000 in the red.

"She simply had no idea what she was doing," Orange said. "She spent and spent and spent."

To top it off, she had siphoned nearly a million dollars from the dealership account, funding the boutique and her own shopping sprees.

"She's robbing you blind," the accountant said. "You should go to the police."

"I'll take care of it," Shellard said. "Let me handle it."

Shellard began to take action. He informed his bank that he wanted Shirley removed as the signatory for his automotive dealership. Then he called a meeting with his friend, Eugene Hand and his lawyer Stuart Winston

"She's ripping me off," Shellard said. "The bitch is robbing me blind. She shuttled over $150,000 into her own account."

"You need to call the police," Winston said.

"I'm going to sell her house," Shellard said. "Fuck her. I need to recoup that loss."

Shellard then confronted Shirley about stealing his money. He was livid, demanding to know what she had been doing.

"He obviously felt betrayed," Orange said. "He was crazier than a shithouse rat, but let's face it, the guy had been good to her. He bought her everything she wanted and let her join him in this decadent lifestyle. But it wasn't good enough for her. She stole his credit cards. Wrote checks in his name payable to her."

Shirley didn't feel remorse at the dressing down by Shellard. She just didn't want the gravy train to leave.

THAT MONEY AIN'T GOING NOWHERE

Shirley began looking for a solution. She noticed a scraggly, down and out woman visiting her boutique often and a light bulb went on her head.

The woman was named Sophia.

Sensing she was a person with some wrong side of the street connections, Shirley saw Sophia and her boyfriend Stanley as "useful idiots" in a plot to kill her husband. They were low-level drug dealers willing to do anything for a buck.

Even if it included murder.

"Shirley gave them a song and dance about how she was an abused spouse," Orange said. "She told the two junkies that she had to endure nightly beatings and rapes. How Shellard would tie her up and have his way with her."

Sophia and Stanley, despite being heroin addicts and petty criminals, felt moral indignation.

Then Shirley waved a few thousand dollars in their face and they were willing to do whatever she asked.

On May 6th, 2005, Shirley lead the two junkies into Shellard's home.

"He's sound asleep in his bed until Shirley attacks him, placing a pillow case over his head," Orange said. "The two junkies hold Shellard down but he begins to fight. He struggles with Sophia and bites her finger. The junkie screams and takes some kind of heavy object from the bedside table and smashes Shellard over the head with it."

Shellard is knocked unconscious but that is when Shirley goes to work.

She takes a needle and injects him with heroin as she wants to make everything look like an overdose.

Then they pulled down his pants.

"Shellard is starting to come to," Orange said. "Then they shove a suppository up his rectum. Oxycontin. This coupled with the heroin is a powerful mix as he has a heart condition. A knock on the head, a shot of heroin and some Oxycontin shoved up his ass killed the man."

Peter is left for dead as Shirley lets some time pass before she calls the police.

A BAD ACTRESS AND A PAIR OF BUNGLING CRIMINALS

Shirley then conjures up her best Meryl Streep act as she calls the police and tells them that she has found Shellard dead on the floor.

"He was into rough sex," she blubbered. "I don't know who could have done this to him."

Police arrived and found the dead Shellard with a towel covering his genitals. His ankles were handcuffed and he was wearing a mouth gag. He also had dog leads, electrical cords and ropes tied around him.

Unfortunately for Shirley, however, the two junkies she hired were not exactly professionals.

A fingerprint sweep led police to Sophia.

Her print had been found on a hallway telephone. They would also find her DNA on a partially smoked cigarette in the kitchen.

The police would track down Sophia as well as her junkie boyfriend. They both confessed to the crime.

"I did it," Stanley said the moment he took a seat in the interrogation room. "Well, I should say that I helped them do it. Shirley drove me and Sophia to the mansion. She wanted him tied up because he had forced her to do bondage with him. Bondage! The dude had frozen all her accounts and was trying to sell her house behind her back. She told him that she wanted to sign some papers so that she could get her house back."

Stanley described the evening of the killing as a casual night on the town. He stated that Shirley took Sophia and himself to a hotel for some gambling.

"We played the poker machines," Stanley told the police. "Then we got some heroin and went to the mansion. Shirley had a syringe of heroin. She went into his bedroom and stuck him with it."

Shellard's daughters, all decent young women, were in shock at what happened to her father. Shirley took it upon herself to try and comfort Jenny but didn't mince words about the kind of man he was.

"Your father was into bondage," Shirley said to her after she tried to sell the police on the fact that Shellard's death was likely due to rough sex. "We never hurt each other, though."

"After my dad died, I confided in Shirley for support," Jenny said. "I thought that she would be the only one who could possibly understand the pain I was going through because she was going through it too."

Shirley didn't know that while she was talking daily on the phone with Jenny, the police had her phone tapped.

They would find out that Shirley was calling around asking for a hitman.

Setting up a sting, they assigned an undercover officer for the operation.

A HITMAN COMETH

Shirley made it known that she was looking for someone to "off" both Sophia and Stanley, thereby getting rid of her only witnesses.

An undercover officer, code-named "Victor" called Shirley and set up four meetings.

"Can you get me pictures of them?" Victor asked.

"No," Shirley said. "But I can get you their address."

"What do they do for a living?"

"They don't 'do' anything," Shirley scoffed. "They're fucking junkies. They sit around all day and shoot heroin."

"Why do you want them killed?"

"They were responsible for killing my husband," Shirley said. "I want them both taken care of."

"It will cost you ten thousand dollars," Victor said. "I need three grand up front. Down payment."

"No problem."

"I need you to get as specific as you can," the hitman said. "Do you want it to be quick or do you want them to suffer?"

"Yes," Shirley said, her eyes cold.

"But do you want them dead?" the hitman asked again. "Or in a wheelchair for the rest of their lives?"

"I want them both dead," Shirley said with finality. "Dead."

Shirley would be arrested and charged with Shellard's murder while the two junkies would receive six years in jail for manslaughter.

In 2007, however, Shirley would elect to go to trial. In her appeal, she somehow convinced the judge that she didn't mean to kill Shellard. She only meant to teach him a lesson.

Shirley would be sentenced to thirteen years in prison which could be lessened to nine years with good behavior.

At the time of this writing, Shirley has become eligible for parole.

A FINAL BETRAYAL

The story took another turn for the bizarre when trustees of Vera Moore's estate would claim that millions of dollars that Moore gave Shellard were meant as a loan and not a gift.

They argued that it should be repaid.

Moore had died eight years prior to Shellard being murdered. He had been a good friend of her son, Kenneth, who died in a car crash in 1972.

Moore then took a shine to the young Shellard, treating him as if he were her own son.

She would give him her son's Waring Bros Tourer Rolls-Royce. In return, Shellard would keep the elderly widow company. He would take her out of her suburban nursing home and drive her around in the Rolls-Royce while they would go out for tea.

"By all accounts," Orange said. "He seemed to have been good to her. Like a son. He was soon given the power of attorney for her and looked after her financial affairs."

Shellard would purchase the Rosecraddock mansion in 1984 for $1.4 million. This was done with Moore's money as the title was split between her company, Brenchley Gardens, and Shellard's company then called "Landro."

Shellard would always seem to have bad luck with women, not only while alive but in death as well as even the attorneys for his mother figure in Vera Moore would turn on him.

BONUS STORY : LADY CANNIBAL

Katherine Mary Knight was born to shed blood. Born October 24th, 1955, she has the distinction of being the first Australian woman to be sentenced to life without the possibility of parole when she murdered her de facto husband John Charles Thomas Price, born 6 January 1955, in Aberdeen, New South Wales, Australia. The murder itself is not necessarily the stuff of horror films or nightmares with extreme heinousness even though Knight did, in fact, stab Price 37 times. Knight's subsequent defilement of Price's body following the murder was extremely atrocious and, as such, was the fundamental reason she received a life without parole sentence. So heinous, in fact that her file is marked "never to be released."

After stabbing Price to death, Knight proceeded to utilize her career skills as a butcher in an abattoir (slaughterhouse) to expertly and precisely excise Price's skin from his corpse in one piece which she hung from a meat hook inside an archway of the house before decapitating him and boiling his head with some vegetables for dinner. She also cut pieces from the victim's buttocks and cooked those as well, making two dinner plates with vegetables for Price's children. As a result, Knight is often referred to among Australians as the "Black Knight" and Aberdeen—once a charming small community named for Aberdeen, Scotland, located approximately 266 kilometers north-northwest of Sydney with a population slightly less than 1,800 that was known for its picturesque countryside, abattoirs, and as the birthplace of the blue heeler cattle dog—is now permanently blemished by Katherine Knight and her heinous crime.

Early Life

Knight was born at Tenterfield Hospital in Aberdeen, New South Wales, Australia, to Barbara Roughan (nee Thorley) who already had four boys—Patrick, Martin, Neville, and Barry—from a prior marriage and another son, Charlie, with her current lover and Katherine's father Ken Knight, an abattoir slaughterman. Barbara was forced to move to another town following cultivating a relationship with Ken, one of her then-husband's co-workers. This relationship was a scandal because of both families' renown within the town. At the time, Jack Roughan had four children and while his two older ones stayed with him and Barbara, the two younger ones were sent to Sydney to live with an aunt. Barbara then gave birth to twins Katherine and Joy, with Joy a half an hour older than Katherine. When the twins were four, Jack died and his two older children moved in with the Knights.

Knight had a troubling upbringing, to say the least. Due to her maternal great-grandmother's Aboriginal heritage and the overwhelming racism in the area at that time, the resulting tension was difficult for all of the children. As a result, Knight was a relatively isolated child; the only people with whom she was close were her twin sister and her Uncle Oscar Knight who, tragically, committed suicide in 1969. Following this heartbreak, the Knights moved back to Aberdeen.

Compounding her isolation, Knight had to contend with an alcoholic father who resorted to intimidation and violence regularly. It is reported that Ken would sexually assault Barbara as many as ten times per day. Barbara shared intimate details of her sex life and her contempt for men and sex with both Katherine and Joy. Further—as if the aforementioned was not enough—Knight claimed repeated sexual abuse by several family members (not her father, though) until she was 11 years old. Despite psychiatrists believing that this did occur, specific details are in doubt. Nonetheless, it is generally widely-accepted that she did suffer said abuse.

Amidst all of this turmoil in her life, everyone who knew her as a child said that while Knight was a generally pleasant girl who earned recognition and awards for her good behavior she did experience uncontrollable rages in response to seemingly minor upsets. During her high school years at Muswellbrook High School she was remembered by former classmates as a bully who attacked at least one student with a weapon and also assaulted a teacher who, in self-defense, injured Knight.

Knight ultimately left school at 15, virtually illiterate. She was, however, able to obtain employment in a clothing factory as a fabric cutter. One year later, at the age of 18, she began working at the local abattoir where her job was to decapitate the pigs; something in which she took great interest and pleasure, often watching the pigs having their throats slit before they reached her. Whereas some of her coworkers thought her behavior to be rather macabre, they just chalked it up to her taking an interest in all aspects of her employer's function. Soon thereafter she secured what she called her "dream job" as an offal (animal organs) cutter at the abattoir. Not long after this Knight was promoted to boner and given her very own set of razor-sharp butcher knives; what she called her most prized possessions. Knight—at every place she ever lived—hung her knives on a nail above her bed so, according to her, they "would always be handy if [she] needed them."

When one, after the fact, examines Knight's early life there are many indications that she would have likely snapped and resorted to murder. If people would have not chalked her erratic behavior up to her "normal" state and reported her disturbing behavior perhaps much of her mayhem could have been prevented.

A Series of Failed Relationships

David Kellett

Knight met her first husband, 22-year old truck driver and hard-drinking David Stanford Kellett in 1973 and as soon as Knight turned 18 she moved in with him. The relationship was one where Knight wore the proverbial pants. If Kellett got into a fight due to his drinking, Knight would be there to use her fists, if necessary, to back him up. In fact, throughout Aberdeen Knight was known for "offering armed combat to anyone who upset her."

Despite her domination of him, Kellett agreed to marry Knight in 1974—at her request. Her mother told Kellett on their wedding day that he had better watch Knight "or she'll fuc*ing kill you." She warned him that if he said or did the wrong thing, cheated on her, or otherwise stirred her up that Knight would not hesitate to kill him. Barbara also told Kellett that her daughter had "a screw loose somewhere." He didn't have to wait long to find this out for himself. On their wedding night after Kellett fell asleep after having sex with Knight only three times, she tried to strangle him for failing to perform to her expectations.

Things progressed from bad to worse with a pregnant Knight burning all of Kellett's clothing and shoes before assaulting him with a frying pan to the back of his head after he came home late from a darts competition at a local pub. Kellett sustained a fractured skull from the altercation and while he initially wanted to press charges against her, Knight—in her loving, best behavior—got him to change his mind. In fact, Kellett was so afraid of his wife that he secretly sought medical care the following day at work.

In May 1976 Knight gave birth to the couple's first child; a daughter named Melissa Ann. Shortly thereafter Kellett tired of Knight's possessiveness and domineering, violent behavior and left her for another woman. The pair fled to Queensland which, as would be expected, did not sit well with his wife. The next day, Knight was seen violently pushing Melissa in a pram down the main street, shaking it roughly from side to side and also stole an axe from a neighbor's back yard and swung it about her head threatening to kill random people. Subsequently, Knight was admitted into St. Elmo's Hospital in Tamworth where she received a diagnosis of postpartum depression. She remained in the hospital for several weeks. Shortly after her release, she left two-month old Melissa on railway tracks soon before a train was expected to arrive. If it wasn't for a homeless man who was known around town as "Old Ted" foraging near the tracks and who heard Melissa crying, the baby would have been killed. Arrested for her negligence, Knight was sent back to St. Elmo's but signed herself out the following day.

Within a week Knight cut the face of local teenager 16-year old Margaret Macbeth with one of her precious knives and ordered the woman to drive her to Queensland to find Kellett. Macbeth escaped when they stopped at a service station and by the time police arrived Knight was threatening a small boy she had taken hostage with her knife. Police disarmed her by attacking her with brooms and she was subsequently admitted into the Morisset Psychiatric Hospital where she told anyone who would listen to her how she was frequently abused by Kellett. She also informed the nurses that she was planning to kill the service station mechanic because he had fixed Kellett's car which then allowed him to leave with his new girlfriend. Knight added that she had planned to murder both Kellett and his mother when she reached Queensland.

After finding out about his wife's plans and disturbing behavior Kellett left his new girlfriend and he and his mother moved to Aberdeen to take care of Knight who was released on 9 August 1976 into their care. Knight, Kellett, and Kellett's mother subsequently moved to Woodridge, a suburb of Brisbane, where Knight was overjoyed to find work at the Dinmore Meatworks in nearby Ipswich.

Shortly thereafter, another example of her ability to attack without provocation involved a local police officer who Knight stabbed but—as was the case with every prior assault—she was never charged. Kellett also recounted another incident wherein he awakened one morning to find Knight straddling his chest grazing his throat with one of her knives. He said that she just laughed at him and stated how easy it would have been for her to kill him. An informative omen, to say the least.

Despite all of the disturbing behavior Knight displayed, Kellett got her pregnant again and on 6 March 1980 little Natasha Maree was born; however, in 1984 the marriage completely disintegrated due to Knight's constant jealousy of Kellett's truck driving job and relentless allegations of his having girlfriends everywhere and she ultimately left him, moving in with her parents back in Aberdeen for a short while before renting a house on McQueen Street in nearby Muswellbrook where she returned to her prior job at the abattoir. Kellett learned of this by returning home from work one night to an empty house.

In 1985, Knight injured her back and was subsequently placed on disability where she received a disability pension. Soon thereafter, Knight again moved back to Aberdeen where she and her daughters lived in a Housing Commission house.

David Saunders

In 1986, Knight met 38-year old divorced miner David Saunders who, a few months after that, moved in with Knight and her daughters while simultaneously maintaining his own apartment in Scone. Saunders was smitten with Knight even knowing full well that she had several "shortcomings" such as attacking people with kitchen appliances, knives, and her fists, but he could not overlook the fact that she was cheerful and charming and possessed a voracious sexual appetite. As would be expected, Knight was extremely jealous about why he kept his apartment and accused him repeatedly of cheating on her. Knight repeatedly threw Saunders out of the house and he returned to Scone each time. Invariably she would seek him out and beg him to come back, which he did.

In May 1987 Knight slit the throat of Saunders' two-month old dingo puppy in front of him as an example of what she would do to him if he ever cheated on her. She then hit Saunders in the head with a frying pan, knocking him unconscious.

Not unlike Kellett, despite all of Knight's violence and unpredictability, in June of the following year, Knight gave birth to Saunders' and her daughter Sarah. Saunders put a deposit on a house that Knight paid off in 1989 with her workers' compensation settlement. Disturbingly, Knight heavily decorated the family house with animal pelts, skulls, leather jackets and old boots, machetes, rusty animal traps, horns, rakes, and pitchforks. And as usual, her butchering knives were hung on the wall above the de facto marital bed.

Another altercation between Knight and Saunders occurred that resulted in Knight hitting Saunders in the face with an iron prior to stabbing him in the stomach with scissors. Of course, he moved back to his Scone apartment during which time Knight had cut up all of his clothes; something he discovered upon his return. She also vandalized his car and attempted suicide by overdosing on sleeping pills which led to her being admitted into yet another psychiatric hospital. This was the last straw and, subsequently, Saunders took a long leave of absence from work and went into hiding. Knight tried to find him but nobody admitted to her whether or not he or she knew where Saunders was. When he tried to return to visit his daughter, Knight had already reported to the police that she was afraid of him and was issued an Apprehended Violence Order (AVO)—similar to a restraining order in the United States—against him.

John Chillingworth

In 1990, Knight became pregnant by 43-year old abattoir worker—and her former coworker—John Chillingworth. In 1991 she gave birth to a boy named Eric. Not surprisingly, from the beginning of their relationship volatility ensued. Chillingworth, a recovering alcoholic, did admit that he struck Knight once after she had pushed him too far after hitting him in the face, knocking his glasses off his face and breaking his dentures in his mouth. Their relationship lasted three more years before she left him for yet another man; a man with whom she had been having an affair for some time: John Price.

John Price

John "Pricey" Price already had three children when he met and began an affair with Knight. He was very well-liked and everyone who knew him described him as a "terrific bloke" whose own marriage ended in 1988. He had custody of his two older children while their then-two-year old daughter went to live with his ex-wife. Even though

Price was well aware of Knight's volatile reputation he still began an affair with her and in 1995 she and her children moved into his house. As was the case with all of her relationships, Price's and hers started out great; he had a steady, well-paying job in the local mines and her children liked him. However, their violent arguments—often precipitated by excessive alcohol consumption—intensified.

In 1998, Knight and Price argued because he refused to marry her so, in true retaliatory Katherine Knight form, she exacted revenge by videotaping items he had allegedly stolen from work and subsequently sending the tape to his boss. Even though the items consisted of out-of-date first aid kits that he found in the company's trash dumpster, Price was fired from the job he had worked for 17 years. Logically, Price kicked Knight out of his house and as she moved back to her own house the news of her actions quickly spread throughout the sleepy town.

Not unlike Knight's former lovers, Price couldn't stay away from her. Despite her horrible temper and violent streak, when she was loving and kind she was the perfect partner. Even though they restarted their relationship he refused to permit her to move back into his house. Of course, the fighting intensified because Knight did not have complete control over him. Additionally, because of his choice to continue to be with her Price lost many of his friends and acquaintances who refused to have anything to do with him while they were together.

In February 2000, Knight's assaults on Price increased, culminating with her stabbing him in the chest. Again, he kicked her out of his house and on 29 February he stopped by the Scone Magistrate Court on his way to work and took out an AVO on Knight—actually after discussing his fears with Knight's first husband, David Kellett—to keep her away from both him and his children. Price was able to secure new employment with Bowditch and Partners Earth Moving and was promoted to supervisor after 12 months and told his boss and coworkers that afternoon that if he failed to come to work the next day to expect that Knight had killed him. Despite his coworkers and boss urging him to not go back to her—even offering to let him stay with them—his worry for his children made him decline their gracious invitations. This would be the worst decision of his life.

When Price arrived home, his children were gone as Knight sent them to a friend's house for a sleepover. He spent a relaxing evening with the neighbors before retiring for the night at approximately 11:00 p.m. Knight arrived at Price's house later that night with the brand new black lingerie she had purchased earlier that day. Also earlier that day, Knight had videotaped herself singing nursery rhymes and hugging and kissing her children while making strange comments; the tape would later be referred to as some type of crude will in which she talked about hoping to be able to see them again. At Price's house, Knight watched television, took a shower, and climbed into his bed where she awakened him and the two of them had sex. Price fell back asleep afterward.

The Crime

Price was awakened by the first of 37 stab wounds Knight inflicted upon him with one of her prized, razor-sharp butcher knives. According to autopsy results, many of the wounds punctured vital organs. Blood evidence at the scene demonstrates that Price did, in fact, attempt to escape from Knight's attack and he actually managed to get to the front door—being repeatedly stabbed the entire time—before he was dragged back into the hallway where he finally exsanguinated and perished.

As if the brutal murder was not enough, what Knight did after Price died was extremely heinous and unbelievable.

After Price was dead, Knight skinned his body and hung the pelt—completely intact—from a meat hook through the head above an archway in his house. Interestingly, she left a small, one-inch square of skin intact upon his body that contained a scar from where she had previously stabbed him. Knight's skinning of Price's skin was so expertly done that following his autopsy, it was able to be reattached to his body in a manner indicative of a clear and appropriate methodology; thus underscoring Knight's adeptness due to her years of experience in the abattoir, likely coupled with her macabre fascination with knives, death, and similar topics.

She then decapitated him and placed his skinned head in a big stock pot on the stove with vegetables. The pot was still warm when police arrived the following morning. Knight also cooked parts of Price—later identified as his buttocks—and served them up as "steak" on two plates with zucchini, squash, cabbage, pumpkin, potatoes, and gravy atop the dinner table. Each plate had beside it a spiteful note for each of Price's children. Knight, apparently, was going to serve the children their own father for dinner. Another "meal" was found in the back yard with some speculating that it was for the dog and others conjecturing that Knight intended to consume parts of her lover but could not bring herself to eat it and discarded it.

She then returned to Price's headless and skinless corpse and arranged his body on the floor with his left arm resting atop an empty 1.25-liter Shelley's Club Lemon Squash soft drink bottle, his legs crossed, and a blood-stained, 31-centimeter yellow plastic-handled knife that matched the type of knife used to commit the heinous act by his right hand.

She also left a handwritten, blood-stained and flesh-covered note atop a picture of Price that read, *"Time you got back Johnathon for rapping [raping] my douter [daughter]. You to Beck [Price's daughter] for Ross—for Little John [Price's son]. Now play with little Johns Dick John Price."* [sic] What Knight hoped to accomplish by penning this note is unknown and all of the accusations were proven to be baseless.

Knight has repeatedly claimed that she has no memory of what happened that fateful night after she and Price had sex.

Price's neighbor became concerned that his work vehicle was still in his driveway at 6:00 a.m. the following morning. Similarly, Price's employer was worried when he failed to arrive at work and sent a coworker to check on him. When the two men saw blood on the front door they called the police who arrived at Price's house at approximately 8:00 a.m. When police entered the house they were met with a grisly crime scene and discovered Knight on the bed comatose from attempting suicide with sleeping pills. After she had killed him, Knight drove to an Aberdeen ATM and withdrew $1,000 from Price's account and then swallowed the pills.

The police officers who found the macabre crime scene at 84 Andrews Street in Aberdeen testified that Knight had skinned Price so methodically that his entire skin—including face, ears, scalp, neck, and even his genitals—was completely intact and resembled that of a "macabre suit" only someone with her abattoir knowledge could achieve. Detective Senior Constable Peter Anthony Muscio issued the complete report that detailed the condition of Price's body, the tremendous amount of blood spatter and pooling throughout the house which indicated that Price did, in fact, fight vehemently for his life, and the gruesome discovery in the kitchen.

The crime scene was so disturbing, so utterly distressing, that many experienced police officers and forensic personnel assigned to the crime scene took stress leave soon after the investigation was completed. Some even admit to still suffering from elements of posttraumatic stress disorder suffered as a result. Even Knight's first husband, Kellett, admitted that he cried for days thinking about what she did and this was compounded by the fact that he had met and spoken to Price shortly before his demise. Kellett still fears for his life even though Knight will never be free again.

The Trial

Knight initially offered to plead guilty to manslaughter and, rightfully, was rejected. She was arraigned on 2 February 2001 for murder to which she pled not guilty. The trial was originally to commence on 23 July 2001 but was later reset for 15 October 2001 due to her attorney's illness. When the trial began, Justice Barry O'Keefe offered to excuse any of the 60 potential jurors who so desired due to the extremely graphic and disturbing photographic evidence that would be brought up during the trial. Five accepted. Several more asked to be excused when the witness list was revealed. Judge O'Keefe adjourned the trial after being informed that Knight wanted to change her plea to guilty and ordered a psychiatric evaluation that night to determine whether Knight understood the ramifications of a guilty plea and was legally sane to do so. Whereas Knight's attorneys initially planned to offer a defense of amnesia and dissociation—which the majority of psychiatrists supported—she was found to be legally sane despite what some psychiatrists thought to be the dominance of her primitive conscience; one that was ruled by the violence, incest, pedophilia, and rape that permeated her childhood. Knight had experienced more sex and violence than love throughout her life and the former dominated her relationships with others, particularly men. The speculation surrounding this proposed defense strategy was that Knight attempted to eat part of Price but the abhorrence she experienced caused her to dissociate from reality and to block everything out of her memory.

The next morning Knight changed her plea to guilty and the empaneled jury was dismissed. As there was no reason given why Knight changed her plea, it was speculated that when confronted with the horror of what she did when shown the crime scene photographs she wanted to spare jurors the similar horror of having to hear all of the gruesome details.

There is much comment in the literature that those who saw Knight sitting at the defense table admitted that she did not look like the vindictive monster that she truly was. It was well-known that she was not someone to cross and ex-lovers and family members testified at her trial that Knight was someone fully capable of considerable violence, even though when not in a murderous rage Knight was the perfect mother and housewife. Chillingworth testified about the incident where Knight killed his puppy and the story of how she got Price fired over an alleged stolen first aid kit was also introduced. Once all of the witnesses were finished testifying the general consensus was that her looks were not to be taken as fact and that someone far more dangerous lurked beneath her seemingly calm exterior. Knight's over-the-top mental and physical vindictiveness demonstrated—to many experts—her vehement belief in revenge and an overdeveloped sense of entitlement. She was also described as one who delighted in making people afraid of her and that she was incapable of true love and empathy as she did not receive either as a developing child. Additional speculation suggested that Knight had fantasized about killing a human being for years and when she did, took considerable pride in her "work"—her ultimate "triumph."

Once Price went to see the police to obtain an AVO against Knight, prosecutors argued that at this moment she put her murderous plot into motion as evidenced by purchasing new lingerie to wear while she seduced him, ensuring that her knives were sharp enough, and making sure that she had the right pots handy for his head. Psychiatrists and criminal profilers asserted that she derived great pleasure from the planning and her subsequent action.

At her trial, one of Australia's foremost criminal psychologists, Dr. Rod Milton, presented his findings following Knight's interview and asserted that she suffered from borderline personality disorder. Borderline personality disorder is a serious mental illness responsible for mood instability, unstable behavior, and typically stormy relationships. It usually affects more women and begins during adolescence or early adulthood. Those who suffer from the disorder commonly have serious problems regulating thoughts and emotions, act impulsively and oftentimes recklessly, and experience very unstable relationships—all of these traits occurred in droves with Knight. Additional symptoms prevalent in individuals with borderline personality disorder include fear of abandonment; an unstable self-image or confused self-identity; self-damaging behaviors such as excessive spending, promiscuity, substance abuse, reckless driving, or binge eating; self-injury or suicidal behavior or ideations; very random and often violent mood swings; a constant feeling of sadness or worthlessness; anger problems to include frequent loss of temper and/ or physical altercations; and paranoia or loss of contact with reality. Those who knew Knight would likely say that she possessed virtually every single one of these qualities. Her extreme fear of abandonment led to her volatile temper and resultant physically violent behavior with her lovers, she attempted suicide on several occasions, her mood swings were frequent and severe, she was very promiscuous which led to her affairs and constant attempts to seduce lovers who had kicked her out, and she regularly consumed a considerable amount of alcohol. Experts link extreme fear of abandonment to the release of adrenaline and norepinephrine which likely account for the trademark severe mood swings and angry outbursts and Knight's continual fear of abandonment and accusations that her lovers were cheating on her resulted in an inordinate amount of these neurotransmitters coursing through her body.

Borderline personality disorder is believed to be an illness with both biological and environmental influences. Heredity and childhood abuse—particularly sexual abuse—have been theorized to be among the strongest predictors of whether someone has a greater predisposition to developing the disorder. Further, the brains of those with borderline personality disorder demonstrate structural abnormalities and resulting malfunction which suggests that the illness has a biological foundation. More specifically, those areas of the brain responsible for emotions and feelings demonstrate higher than average brain activity.

The name borderline personality disorder was originally so named as sufferers were considered to be on the "borderline" between neurosis and psychosis with some professionals asserting that the name was inaccurate. With respect to Knight, that she has frequently been called psychotic may demonstrate some validity in this moniker. The fundamental differences between neuroses and psychoses are that while the former are mild mental disorders, the latter result from gross mental and emotional disruptions to include personality changes; lost or changed contact with reality; projection of certain thoughts upon others; loss of the ego to the id; disorganized, bizarre, and irrational thought processes; and frequent hospitalization due to attempted suicide and/or other self-harming behaviors. Whereas the literature suggests that individuals with borderline personality disorder experience some alleviation of their impulsivity and volatility when they reach their 40's, such was not the case with Knight.

Another speculation regarding Knight's psychological nature involves piquerism, defined as sexual arousal by cutting or stabbing another's skin, sometimes resulting in death. The literature defines piquerism as a form of paraphilic sadism which can range from a single prick, to multiple stab wounds to an eroticized area, to elaborate cutting, stabbing, or mutilation; with the last eerily similar to Knight's treatment of Price's deceased body. Piquerism is closely associated with so-called "lust murders" in which the offender stabs or mutilates the victim. Other common attributes associated with piquerism include posing or propping of the deceased's body, inserting items into various bodily cavities, anthropophagy (eating flesh or consuming blood), and necrophilia. Knight did, in fact, pose Price's corpse and planned to feed his flesh to his children and, perhaps, attempted to consume some herself. Prevalence of this disorder is currently unknown.

Sentencing

At her sentencing hearing on 9 November 2001, despite having pled guilty, Knight never accepted responsibility for her actions in Price's death. At this hearing, Knight's legal team requested her removal from the courtroom so she wouldn't have to listen to all of the details that she had allegedly forgotten which was adamantly denied and she was given the harshest sentence allowed under Australian law. When Dr. Timothy Lyons—the medical examiner who conducted Price's autopsy—took the stand and described every single gory detail, Knight became hysterical and required sedation.

According to Dr. Lyons, Price, thankfully, was already dead when he was skinned. The skinning was conducted professionally with the razor sharp knife inserted beneath his collarbone and sliced across to the other shoulder before being cut down Price's chest, over his stomach to his pubic area where a "T" was cut so the knife sliced down the front of his legs to his feet before moving the knife back up his body, skinning the back of his arms and the top of his head before peeling the victim's skin off in one piece, exposing his intestines. The skin displayed every single one of Knight's 37 stab wounds. Price's head was then removed with a clean cut at the C3-C4 juncture just above his shoulders. Dr. Lyons stated that the entire process would have taking approximately 40 minutes. Further, Dr. Lyons testified that the myriad wounds entered Price's aorta, both of his lungs, his liver, his stomach, his pancreas, his colon, and left kidney that had part of it completely sliced off.

Just prior to handing down Knight's sentence, Justice O'Keefe said of Price that *"The last minutes of his life must have been a time of abject terror for him as they were a time of utter enjoyment for her...she has not expressed any contrition or remorse and if released she poses a serious threat to the security of society."* Knight was given a life sentence without the possibility of parole and became the first woman in Australia's history with the distinction of having her file marked "never to be released." Of particular interest was that Australia had no statutory prohibition to the defilement Knight committed against Price's corpse which precluded her being charged with additional crimes. Her actions were so out of the scope of the law that it was likely unbelievable that someone could do something like this to another human being.

Evidence of her premeditation was further indicated when she said to one of Price's daughters "I told him if he took me back this time it was to the death."

Post-Conviction

In June 2006, Knight appealed her life sentence, asserting that life without the possibility of parole was too severe for murder; however a three-judge panel in the New South Wales Court of Criminal Appeal consisting of Justices Peter McClellan, Megan Latham, and Michael Adams dismissed her petition in September of that same year citing that her crime was so appalling and "almost beyond contemplation in a civilized society." Justice McClellan stated during her appeal that "*The psychiatric evidence indicates that her personality is unlikely to change in the future and, if released, she would be likely to inflict serious injury or perhaps death on others.*"

It has been alleged that Knight was inspired the horror film *Resurrection* (1999) in which a serial killer tried to reconstruct the body of Christ with parts of his victims. There is some speculation that Knight was a copycat of sorts of a gruesome scene in which a body was killed, decapitated, and then skinned and hung on a meat hook.

SO DAMN EVIL

GERALDINE PAGE

Louise Melanie "Louise" May was looking for a place to stay.

She had three children but had them taken away as the courts declared her to be an unfit parent because of her drug addiction. At the age of 23, she needed to get her life back together.

Things seemingly could not get any worse for the recovering addict.

But then she arrived at the home of Kerry Dalton seeking help.

"I don't have anywhere to go," Louise said, realizing that her audience in Kerry Lyn Dalton was only half paying attention. "Rob is in jail. They took away my kids. Damn CPS."

The frazzled haired twenty-eight-year-old alternated between staring at the television and smoking on the meth pipe. She took a deep toke on the pipe and let the smoke out.

"You can stay with me," she finally said.

"Oh my God, thank you," Louise said.

"But it is only until Rob gets out," Kerry said.

"I understand. I understand. No problem."

But Louise had a problem. Meth addiction.

Now she had added another problem in Kerry Lyn Dalton.

"Kerry was a queen in the subculture of meth and alcoholism if there is such a thing," forensic psychologist Greta Smith said. "She had been married twice and had five children by three different men. It was amazing how Kerry Dalton even survived to the age of 28. Unemployable, she was the epitome of a bully and would do anything to get her way. She had little regard for the rights or feelings of other people, running roughshod over everyone in her path."

Unfortunately for Louise, she had gotten in Kerry's way.

Kerry would be arrested for drug possession and hauled off to jail for a short stint. She had been Louise's supplier and Louise needed her fix.

But she had no money.

So she began pawning off things she found around the house during a spur of the moment "garage sales." Some of Kerry's old jewelry would be sold off in exchange for drugs.

But when Kerry was released from prison and found out that her stuff had been pawned off, she became more than livid.

She became homicidal.

"Kerry took the theft as a personal affront," Smith said. "This was a fragile living situation between two drug addicts. Junkies. They had little regard for one another and really see each other as utilities to use or supply drugs. Louise is willing to sell out Kerry's stuff while Kerry is willing to kill Louise to gain revenge."

On June 26th, 1988, Kerry confronted Louise at the mobile home. Three other people in their drug dealing clique soon arrived, Mark Lee Tompkins, Sheryl Baker and another transient named "George".

Kerry ordered Louise to sit down and tied her to a chair. She then began torturing her, splicing off and electrical cord and burning her with it.

Louise screamed in pain.

Tompkins then began joining in the torture, jabbing at the defenseless Louise with a screwdriver.

The two then demanded that Sheryl partake in the abuse as well. Reluctantly, Sheryl complied.

"Sheryl felt as if they would have killed her if she didn't do as she was told," Smith said.

After the course of a few hours, the three then took turns torturing Louise.

Kerry enjoyed shocking her captive with the electric cord, laughing as Louise screamed. Seeking to raise the stakes, her boyfriend took an iron skillet and smashed it against the back of Louise's head.

"They hit her with such force that it made a dent in the pan," Smith said.

Kerry's sadism was still not satiated. She kept thinking of different ways to torture Louise then came up with the idea to inject her with some battery acid. Her boyfriend got a syringe and they plunged the battery acid into her vein as well as poured it down her throat.

"Kerry was a sadist," Smith said. "She justified her torture of Louise to the fact that the woman sold a few items of her jewelry and got maybe twenty-five bucks for it."

Tompkins then put Louise out of her misery by stabbing her in the neck with the screwdriver. She fell to the ground and he began stomping on her head until she died.

What happened to Louise's body after remains shrouded in mystery and hearsay.

Later that evening, a sheriff arrived at the mobile home on a burglary call. He saw no evidence of a burglary but did describe one of the residents, Joann Fedor, as high on meth. The sheriff then inspected the exterior and interior of the mobile home, finding nothing.

The disappearance of Louise remained unsolved for three years until Sheryl Baker had a crisis of conscience. She confessed to the crime, telling the authorities of what happened the day Louise was killed. In return for her confession, the authorities allowed her to plead to second-degree murder.

One of Louise's cousins stated on-line that the prosecuting attorney told her that one of trio involved admitted that they dismembered the body of Louise. They then spread the body parts out across different locations on different Indian reservations.

"For meth heads," Smith said. "They certainly knew what they were doing when disposing of a body. They were all jobless junkies but when it came to murdering someone they were willing to work hard. Damn hard in order to avoid detection. They would have avoided detection but for Sheryl Baker finally coming forward."

Kerry's trial would begin on February 8th, 1995. The judge, Thomas J. Whelan stated that

"I think the record is clear that nobody has ever been found in this case. The record is equally clear that there is circumstantial evidence that there was a homicide. There's also conflicting circumstantial evidence that it may not be a homicide; in fact, she may still be alive ..."

"My reason for making these statements is to establish for the record that in my mind corpus is a legitimate issue in this case. It's not a ruse that - there is a legitimate issue before the jury as to whether or not there's - a corpus of a homicide has been established."

Kerry would never confess to the crime on record and would claim innocence.

"The thing that makes me the most mad is that he is lying, and he knows he's lying," Kerry said of the prosecuting attorney.

The jury foreman, John Castleman, would concede that they found her guilty on the basis of "the type of murder it was" despite a lack of physical evidence to prove that Louise was murdered.

Mark Thompkins would be convicted of first-degree murder.

Kerry Dalton would be sentenced to death on May 23rd, 1995.

"She is the epitome of evil," Smith said. "We can say the drugs did it but there was a lot of premeditation to what she did to poor Louise. If anyone deserves to be on death row and have her execution expedited, it is Kerry Dalton."

Victoria Forbes, however, continues to champion the innocence of her sister.

"She was convicted without a body," Forbes said. "Without a weapon, without any blood evidence, without any physical evidence, without a crime scene, without anyone being declared deceased nearly seven years later as she stood trial with no one declared deceased being charged with the death penalty."

There continued to be some on-line controversy regarding Kerry's guilt as her supporters point to the fact that Louise's husband claims to have had a call from Louise a week after she was murdered.

That "evidence", however, is all they have to go on.

Despite Dalton's persistence at an appeal, it was clear to law officials believe that Kerry Dalton was guilty of the murder of Irene Louise May. Neither Tompkins nor Baker had anything to go after coming forward after three years of silence. They finally sobered up and confessed their crime.

Kerry Dalton did not and is now on death row.

SHEILA LABARRE

RUDOLPH DEETZ

101

PROLOGUE

The farmhouse and surrounding area looked like something from the set of "Little House on the Prairie."

The house on Harvey Farm stood nestled in between tall pine trees, peaceful streams, and wildlife.

A place where you don't expect to find scenes that would be given an "X" rating if it were a horror movie.

The police arrived at the home while conducting a search for a missing young man named Kenneth Countje. They did not have to search far to find evidence of criminal activity. In the front of the property, lay a mattress burning alongside a smoking garbage barrel.

Their first inclination was to believe that the resident was burning garbage. A citation was due, maybe, but they had more pressing matters to attend to.

But upon closer inspection of the barrel, the officers saw a bone sticking out of the garbage.

A femur?

A mass of fleshy goo remained at the knob of the bone and the smell of the charred remains made the policemen gag.

They both gave each other a look of horror. Here in a town where the most serious crime would be a speeding ticket or jaywalking, the police were about to enter a whole world of horror beyond their wildest imagination.

CHAPTER ONE

Epping, New Hampshire.

Population = less than six thousand.

Epping is a rainy, small town that has been sarcastically nicknamed "The Center of the Universe". That has not stopped the residents from hosting parades, canoe races and music festivals. But when Sheila LaBarre arrived, the tiny hamlet soon became known for murder.

"She was a smart woman," forensic psychologist Paula Orange said. "Not book smart but intuitive. She could read people."

Sheila was born Sheila Kaye Bailey in Fort Payne, Alabama in 1958.

She was the youngest of six children. Her first marriage with a man named Ronnie Jennings would last less than two months. Jennings would find out that Sheila had been locking his child from a previous marriage in a closet to punish her. Jennings would divorce Sheila but she would find herself a new man in short order, tying the knot with John Baxter and moving to Chattanooga, Tennessee. Even though married, she would secretly fantasize about being swept away by a rich man. Sheila's mental illness would come to bear in her second marriage and that would end in divorce as well. Despondent, Sheila tried to kill herself and was sent to a psychiatric facility. She would be raped by an orderly inside the hospital.

Now single in Tennessee, the cash-strapped Sheila was forced to live in a local YMCA. She attended a church service and had a private talk with one of the preachers as she wanted "spiritual guidance." She would later claim that the reverend asked if she wanted to "sit in his lap." She then went to a psychiatrist who asked her if she had anal sex with any of her former husbands. The doctor then called Sheila at home and asked if "what she was wearing" and if she "was touching herself."

"If what we are to believe all of Sheila's stories," Orange said. "Then literally all of her interactions with men have ended with them as the pervert and her as the victim. Her sister would later testify that Sheila was molested by her father when she was young. Then her abusive marriages, the rape at the psych facility segues into a spiritual search where she meets a preacher who shows her the tent in his pants. Crazy."

CHAPTER TWO

Sheila turned to personal ads after her failures in marriage. She didn't like the normal courtship process of going to bars and meeting men there. She used the personal ads to cherry pick the men she wanted, men she could dominate.

"Whether on-line or off-line, Sheila behaved like a woman who was in complete control," Orange said. "She would develop a strange kind of power over men. It was almost as if she knew which men would be vulnerable to her feminine wiles and which ones would fight back. But when it came to Dr. Bill LaBarre, it was more of a case of getting the money."

While in Tennessee, Dr. LaBarre decided to take out a personal ad. He would get a response from Sheila who immediately sought to separate herself from the other paramours of the rich doctor.

She sent the doctor nude Polaroids of herself.

The strategy worked.

"She showed no shame in flirting with the older man and soon had him in the palm of her hand," Orange said. "He'd buy her fancy clothes, necklaces, the whole nine yards."

Wilfred "Bill" LaBarre was a successful chiropractor but lonely. Overweight and bespectacled, he had little to offer aside from his wealth. He was in his sixties and recently widowed.

Dr. Labarre was considered a good man by all who knew him. He had been the "Chiropractor of the Year" in 1983 but that would be the same year his beloved Edwina would pass away from cancer. Eager to salve the loneliness, he married another woman named Leona but she abandoned the doctor after a few years. He had two children from his first marriage; Laura and Gregory.

Now alone and widowed, the doctor wanted to spend his golden years enjoying his wealth.

And a young woman.

He would look at the nude Polaroids of the curvaceous Southern Belle, becoming obsessed.

"Here was a lonely, older man who all of a sudden had a 27-year old woman sending him nude photos. He thought he hit the jackpot."

Dr. LaBarre soon invited Sheila to come live with him at his farm in Epping, New Hampshire. The farm was a spacious one, a 115-acre horse ranch that according to LaBarre, "needed a female hand."

Sheila would become enamored by life on the farm, at least at first. She "never heard a June bug before" and the isolated country home gave her a peace that she never experienced.

Neighbors were not shocked that Dr. LaBarre took in such a younger woman as his girlfriend. He reportedly had other girlfriends after his wife died. "Sheila ran all the other girls off," one neighbor said.

But Sheila would prove to be a high-maintenance girlfriend. She would drain Dr. LaBarre's finances, making him buy her gifts and prizes which included a brand-new Silver Mercedes.

She also began to interject herself into LaBarre's estate and business dealings.

The farm that LaBarre owned was called the Old Harvey Farm. It was named after the original owners of the property who still lived in the area. But Sheila forced the doctor to change the name, she wanted it called something that reflected her personality.

The Silver Leopard Farm.

Sheila then had a sign made up and had it placed at the entrance.

She was marking her territory.

CHAPTER THREE

Despite the constant gifts and financial prizes, Sylvia proved to be an ungrateful sugar baby. The relationship would turn tempestuous after a few months. Sheila would claim that Dr. LaBarre often referred to himself as an "old fart" and looked the other way when Sheila began to have different men over for sex.

"He just worried about me when I would date far from home. But he was getting old and his heart would stop beating sometimes."

But the couple fought and police were routinely called to the residence to mediate their domestic disputes.

"You would sometimes hear gunshots," Bruce Allen, a LaBarre neighbor said. "You would hear her screaming, 'I'm going to kill you, you mother fucker!'"

Sheila once pulled a gun on the doctor and forced him out of the home. The chiropractor hid behind a boulder as his girlfriend shot at him.

LaBarre's daughter also recalled that she heard Sheila screaming threats at her father. "I'm gonna kill the horses and I'm going to kill you too."

Laura would later remark at how much her father changed after Sheila came into his life. He went from a normal, well-liked member of the community to a meek, submissive man.

"Sheila was all about being an opportunist," Orange said. "She had the ability to read a man, analyzing his weaknesses, size him up and then push the buttons. With LaBarre, she had a lonely man in front of her. He would tolerate anything in order not to lose her at first and then he simply became fearful of his life. These men in this small New England town did not have the wherewithal to deal with a violent sociopath like Sheila."

Sheila didn't stop with the renaming of Old Harvey Home. She soon took over the accounting duties at LaBarre's chiropractic business. She began organizing the practice into a well-oiled machine. She would track down patients who owed the doctor money and file numerous small claims in the Hampton District Court.

Concerned friends would advise him to dump Sheila before it was too late but it became apparent that the doctor either didn't know how or was afraid to. Dr. LaBarre informed neighbor Bruce Allen that he "had to get rid of her" and that he wanted to "send her back to Alabama. Hopefully, she'll stay there."

Her power over Dr. LaBarre increased to the point where he had given her power of attorney. She began rewriting his will, becoming the executor of his estate. The will stated that he was leaving everything to "a very special lady known as Sheila Kaye Jennings LaBarre."

"The will was very carefully redacted from the original," Orange said. "She kept a lot of the parts of the original and used her own typewriter to amend the little detail of where all the assets will go to. She was very astute and covered her tracks very well for someone who was supposedly schizophrenic."

The two would live together (Sheila would move out briefly but claim to be his common-law wife) from 1987 until LaBarre's death in 2000 at the age of 74. The coroner logged his cause of death as heart disease. There were suspicions among those close to the doctor that believe Sheila poisoned him to hasten the process.

"He was pretty old," Orange said. "And according to the autopsy, the heart disease was significant. So Sheila didn't have anything to do with his death despite the suspicions. The killings would come later."

Sheila would inherit the farm, LaBarre's Chiropractor office, two apartments and a rental home.

This was all valued at over two million dollars in assets.

Strangely, Sheila would marry a Jamaican national named Wayne Ennis in August of 1995 while living with Dr. LaBarre. Ennis drove a tour bus around Jamaica and Sheila made sure that when she toured the islands with Dr. LaBarre that they would cross paths with her Jamaican lover. She arranged for Ennis to obtain a visa and took him back to the farm with her. She would later claim that she and the doctor had stopped having sex and that she "had needs" which apparently Ennis took care of. She would later concede to pleasing the doctor sexually, "I'd use my hand," she said afterward.

Ennis would live in the farmhouse for almost a year. He had his own numerous encounters with Sheila which were violent and bizarre. One night, she ordered him to get in the car. The two then drove around the quiet town, Sheila's voice taking on a conspiratorial tone.

"I wish one of those damn horses would just kick him (Dr. LaBarre) in the head," Sheila said. "Kick him in the head and kill his old ass. I've thought about strangling him myself. But now I have a better idea. I want you to kill him."

Ennis was too frightened to say no to Sheila. The two would eventually divorce and the court records reveal that Sheila took out a restraining order against him.

Ennis disputed the allegations and stated that Sheila was the abuser.

He would later recall being punched, pushed, and shot at by Sheila.

"She told me that she was going to send me back to Jamaica in a box," Ennis said.

Dr. LaBarre told Ennis that Sheila was crazy and believed that she would eventually kill him. He gave the Jamaican money and sent him to the bus station, requesting that he leave town for his own safety.

After the relationship with Ennis ended, Sheila began dating James Brackett.

She and James would remain together for six years despite the fact that Sheila would attack Brackett with a pair of scissors, a machete, and an ax. When all of that failed she tried to shoot him.

The two would break up after which Brackett would get himself a vanity license plate that read "I'm Alive."

Brackett recalled moments where Sheila would act sweet and nice only to go into a violent rage moments later. He said that the greatest example was a time when he was taking a long bath with Sheila only to have her get out of the tub and smash him in the face with a two-foot grill brush.

Two of his teeth would be knocked out from the impact.

Sheila would attack Brackett for a variety of transgressions that would not be guilty of. Hurting her rabbits, damaging her property or having affairs with other women.

Brackett finally had enough, escaping from the farm on one rainy night and hitchhiking back into town.

"I'm lucky to be alive," he would later state.

CHAPTER FOUR

Sheila inherited the farm after LaBarre's death. The doctor's children tried to contest the will but were told that the odds of winning the case were 50/50 at best. They would also have to front over $50,000 to pay for the court costs.

Sheila soon turned the farm into her own private fiefdom. She would hire young men to help her around the place then pay them with her sexual favors or sometimes just beat the shit out of them.

"There would neighbors that would claim to see young men leave her house," Orange said. "They would look beaten up; black eyes, bloody lips, facial contusions. God knows what else."

Her neighbors began to suspect something fishy was going on but had no real evidence to call the police with.

"The first time I met Sheila LaBarre was at the Harvey Farm Stand," said Bonnie Meroth, one of Sheila's neighbors. "It was during the summertime when the produce was ready. I had no basic interaction with her except that of someone standing next to another person as a consumer. And she suddenly turned around and said 'I'll kill you if you come down to my farm' or words to that effect."

Bonnie would later claim that Sheila would try to scare her while driving down the road, nearly running her over while she was on her morning walk.

When she wasn't intimidating neighbors and townsfolk, Sheila would use the farm as the playground for her own private fetishes.

She liked to control and bully men. Stroking one of her pet rabbits, she would punish and insult the men unlucky enough to work at her farm.

"Are you kidding me?" Sheila yelled at the young man who dropped the wheelbarrow. "This should have been done yesterday."

He was young and naive, needing money. If it meant taking lip from Sheila, so be it. He needed work and she seemed nice when she hired him.

"Hurry up!" Sheila said, kicking the man in his buttocks. "Move, move. Are you kidding me? I've never seen a lazier man in my life."

Fatigued after working sixteen hours for seven days straight, the young man keeled over in exhaustion, dropping the wheelbarrow.

"Bitch made, perverted ass pedophile!" Sheila said. "Is this what I am paying you for? I am paying you to work. Now get off your bitch ass. Now!"

It became apparent that Sheila had a gift. A gift of controlling a certain type of man. Verbally abusive and overbearing, she encountered very little resistance.

She kicked the young man again. "Your name is 'bitch', you hear me?"

His real name was Michael Deloge.

CHAPTER FIVE

Deloge had problems as a teen. He got caught up in drugs and found himself on the streets, living out of homeless shelters. In 2004, he would meet Sheila LaBarre.

Deloge became smitten with the woman whom he saw as the life of the party. She would drink beer and play country songs on a guitar. According to Deloge's stepfather, Gordon Boston, the duo would indulge in drugs and study "sadistic material".

Deloge would join Sheila at her farm and soon become her personal whipping boy. Sheila would slap him around like a rag doll. One of the fellow ranch hands, Philip Sullos, recalled witnessing Sheila beating on Deloge with a hardwood stick until he bled. Deloge cowered and took the beating. She would then throw Deloge into a windowless shack and slam the door shut.

Deloge would cower meekly in the corner until Sheila came and got him, making no attempt to escape.

He would be declared missing in 2004 and no one would ever see him again.

In February of 2006, Sheila began looking for a new farmhand. She had her own criteria. He had to be young but pliable to her controlling methods.

She would find the perfect foil in Kenny Countie.

"Kenny was a lovely boy," Carolynn Lodge, Kenny's mother said. "He couldn't do enough for you. Everyone was his friend. I was so proud of him. He never had a horrible word for anybody and that was the problem. He trusted everybody."

Kenny's trust would lead him into Sheila LaBarre's trap.

Kenny would answer one of Sheila's personal ads. The young man was still naive and according to some reports had a "low IQ". The two met through a telephone personal ad service with Sheila calling up the young man and charming him in a way that no woman ever did.

"He (Kenny) told my son Brian that he met a 47-year old woman in New Hampshire," Lodge said. "She owned a farm. She owned a beautiful car. And she was rich. And he was serious about her."

"Kenny fit Sheila's psychological criteria," Orange said. "She targeted men whom she could overpower not only physically but also mentally. She was older than Kenny and light years more cunning. She knows exactly what to say and do to push his buttons. She takes the lead, telling him that he is going to be 'in for the time of his life' and that she 'can't wait to see him.' To a young man with limited experience and intelligence like Kenny, this is music to his ears."

Sheila would arrive at Kenny's home in the silver Mercedes. The silver leopard, the cougar, picking up her prey and taking him back to her lair.

Kenny's family would never see him again.

Sheila would use the same methods on Kenny as she did on the men in the past. She seduced the young man first then isolated him in her farmhouse. Then she berated him verbally before beating the shit out of him with face slaps, punches, and a wooden stick.

The beatings would come to a head during a weekend in February of 2000. Sheila beat Kenny's face into a pulp, took the wooden cane to his legs and may have poisoned him.

Then she decided to take him shopping at Walmart.

Placing him in a wheelchair, she rolled him around the outlet as she stocked up on garden supplies. She dumped two containers of diesel fuel into the prone Kenny's lap.

Little did he know that she would later use the gas to incinerate his body.

Customers gawked at the odd couple, concerned about the contusions on Kenny's face.

"Fuck you looking at?" Sheila would scream as she sped down through the aisle.

Employees of the store soon became concerned, calling the police.

The cops would arrive, confronting the couple in the store. They inquired about Kenny's condition but he didn't respond. Instead, Sheila took the lead, telling Kenny that he "didn't have to talk to these assholes."

The police didn't follow through. Kenny remained silent as Sheila rolled him through the store and out the door. No crime had been witnessed and they let the couple go.

Kenny's mother would later sue the police for negligence but it was tossed out of court in 2010.

A few nights after the Walmart incident, Sheila would make a frantic phone call to the police.

"I got a pervert in my house!" she screamed into the phone. "He's a pedophile! A pedophile!"

In a bizarre sequence of events, Sheila began to play a recording for the detective on the other end. She had routinely audio recorded everything she did, trying to incriminate the young men she worked with into admitting they were pedophiles. On this occasion, she played back a recording of her and Kenny.

"On the tape was my son, vomiting," Lodge said. "He kept saying 'he's faking, he's faking.'"

Sheila would ask Kenny if he was a pedophile on the tape. Kenny would answer 'yes'.

"Now he's a pedophile," Kenny's mother said. "Now he's raping children. Raping his brother. He's vomiting."

The police would write off the call as the rantings of a schizophrenic. They did not immediately respond to the residence.

Sheila would then kill Kenny Countie.

"She had to justify the killing of the young men in her own mind," Orange said. "For some bizarre reason, she would brainwash herself into thinking that her victims were pedophiles. She would repeat the question like a mantra, 'Are you a pedophile? Are you a pedophile?' Working herself up into an angry and violent state of mind before she killed the man."

Sheila's sister, Lynn Noojin, believed that Sheila was sexually abused by her father. Because of this, she became obsessed with child molestation. She would accuse the young men that worked for her of various sexual deviations, including pedophilia, incest, and bestiality.

CHAPTER SIX

After the bizarre call to police, authorities would not arrive at the farmhouse until the next morning. The police would enter the grounds, seeing both the burning mattress and barrel with Kenny's remains. They would not identify the burning bones as belonging to Kenny until much later.

Sheila had murdered Kenny the night before. She attacked Kenny ferociously with a kitchen knife, pushing the already weakened young man to the floor and stabbing away.

Blood sprayed and splattered everywhere.

Sheila then dragged Kenny's body out to her yard where she doused his body with the diesel fuel they had purchased at Walmart.

Lighting a match, she set the dead man on fire. She then took her pet rabbit in her lap, pulled up a chair and watched Kenny Countie burn.

"He was dismembered," Kenny's mother said, fighting tears. "And he was put in a pit and burned. But my son, he just wanted to be loved. I can't imagine what he must have been thinking. Because he was all alone."

Police would look throughout the house and find blood splatter on the walls and floor. A forensic team arrived and matched the blood with Kenny's DNA sample from his Army days. They would find the wallet of Michael Deloge but not his body.

Hundreds of police would spend seventeen days searching the 115-acre property. They found numerous burn pits and blood remains that were so old they had layers of dust on them. They would find clothing that belonged to Deloge and some toes that remain unidentified (it is rumored that the toes may belong to a mysterious Irish man who Sheila claims was stalking her.)

Going on the run from the cops, Sheila hitchhiked along Interstate 293. She was then picked up by Stephen Martello.

"Thanks so much for stopping," Sheila said.

"No problem," Martello said, looking the buxom Southern Belle up and down. His heart began to race.

Will he get lucky?

"My car broke down about two miles back. I got into a fight with my boyfriend and I'm trying to get to Dorchester."

"I'm headed that way," Martello said.

Sheila clutched her purse as if it were a security blanket and she kept looking back at the rear window.

"You all right?" he asked.

"Yeah," Sheila said "Just a little rattled. You know, it has been a tough day."

Martello took Sheila to the drug store when she said she needed to stop off and "buy some things". He tailed Sheila around the store until she bought a douche. Noting her erratic behavior, Martello disappeared out of Sheila's earshot to call the police on his cell phone.

"Hi," Martello said. "Just curious if you folks are looking for someone who just robbed a bank or an escaped mental patient. I just met a woman who is acting kind of strange."

When the authorities informed him that they were not actively investigating someone with that kind of background, Martello took Sheila to a hotel room.

The two would engage in wild and loud sex.

"You just had sex with an angel," Sheila proclaimed after they were done.

"Is that right?"

"You're not like the other men," Sheila said. "My boyfriend, Jesus, I just caught him with a huge stack of child porn. He is a pedophile. So are all those damn cops. Pedophiles, all of them. I think all sex offenders must die."

Martello said nothing. Instead, he put his pants and shoes on as fast as he could as Sheila continued to go on another bizarre rant.

"Vengeance is mine saith the Lord," Sheila said, laying on the bed in post-coital repose. "I was sent back to earth as an angel. I know how to speak to God in Hebrew. Do it every night."

Martello excused himself and high-tailed it out of the hotel room. He arrived home and saw the television broadcast about Sheila. He didn't call the police, worried that he would be an accessory to her crimes. Instead, Martello drove to the station and practically sprinted to the front desk.

"I think I just met Sheila LaBarre."

"To the end, Sheila had control over just about every man put in front of her," Orange said. "Here was a guy who picks her up at the side of the road. He thinks she is crazy enough to where he calls the cops to find out if there are any missing mental patients. He knows that she has a screw loose but he has sex with her anyway. It may be a poor reflection on men for sure but his response is typical. The men that Sheila encountered, from Dr. LaBarre all the way to Stephen Martello, all had the same false narratives going on in their head. They did not see a beautiful woman as something evil. It just didn't fit their narrative. So when Sheila begins her abuse, they just can't believe it. They refuse to hit a 'woman' back. She gets them 'pussy whipped' then beats the shit out of them. Rinse and repeat."

Sheila LaBarre would later be arrested for the murders of Michael Deloge and Kenneth Countje. She would plead no guilty on the grounds of insanity.

"This is a sick, sick woman," her attorney would argue. "Deeply disturbed."

Court-appointed psychiatrists would agree, testifying that Sheila was delusional as well as schizophrenic.

The jury would visit both LaBarre's farm and the Walmart where she frequented first hand. Sheila would join them as well although she was forced to wear a stun belt.

The jury did not buy her insanity defense and found her guilty.

"The fact that she has to remain for the rest of her life behind bars," Kenny's mother said. "She got what she asked for. She'll never see the light of day. Horrible thing is that my son, he's not here with me. He was only twenty-four."

Sheila LaBarre is now serving life in without possibility of parole.

MARRIAGE, MONEY AND MURDER : THE TRUE STORY OF AMY BOSLEY

APRIL PETERS

Amy Pape was born in 1967 and raised in the small town of Alexandria, Kentucky. She grew up poor, the only child of a working mother and an alcoholic father. She excelled in school, however, and received good grades at Campbell County High School. She graduated high school in 1986 and enrolled in business management classes at a local junior college.

"Alexandria was a place of demolition derbys, county fairs, and church," forensic psychologist Jillian Scott said. "Amy wanted more. Her mother was a hard worker. Her father was an alcoholic but doted on Amy. They both wanted a better life for her."

To make ends meet, Amy began working as a waitress. One of her regular customers was a young man named Bob Bosley. He immediately took a shine to the pert Amy and began frequenting the eating establishment just so he could see her.

Bob was then just getting his roofing business started and looked to be a young man going places in life. The kind of man Amy could see herself marrying to rescue her out of the drudgery of life in a small Kentucky town.

But Bob was also known as a party animal, throwing wild get-togethers on his boat in Lake Cumberland.

He would eventually ask Amy out and she would join him during these wild forays, taking her top off along with the rest of the party girls at Bob's disposal.

The two would date for four years until they finally tied the knot.

A daughter named Morgan Nicole was born followed by a son named Trevor three years later.

Domestic bliss seemed to await the Bosley family.

ARCHETYPAL AMERICAN DREAM

Amy loved the high-life that the marriage to Bob allowed her to experience. She was living the life that the majority of her classmates at Campbell County High would be envious of.

Bob Bosley had been the answer to her prayers.

"(He was) someone who could come into her life," M.William Phelps said. "Give her what she wanted and she didn't have too give much back."

The partying lifestyle would continue, a double life of sorts as the couple would have house parties in the mansion, sipping champagne and romping in the backyard pool.

But then they would go to church on Sunday...

"Amy Bosley was all about the money," Scott said. "That was her sole criterion in seeking out a mate. She didn't care about looks, kindness, personality, character, none of that. If the man had money, it was a go."

And Bob Bosley had money.

Bob had now single-handedly built one of the largest chimney sweep and roofing businesses in the region. He was a "go-to" business leader in the community of Alexandria.

"He would often donate his services to churches," said journalist Jim Hannah. "To install steeples."

Bosley played the role of the conservative, Christian man to the community at large. He wanted to do right by everyone, especially his family as he took pride in providing for their every need.

The Bosleys had everything on the surface. Bob had purchased sports cars, horses, a private plane and a 50-foot yacht.

He had no idea, however, that Amy Bosley wanted more than he could provide.

A lot more.

"Big house," Phelps said. "Big cars. Money in the bank. She didn't have to work if she didn't want to but that's not enough. That's not enough for her. She wants it all."

Things were going so well for the couple financially that Bob moved the family out of their home and had everyone stay in their weekend luxury cabin. He did this while a new castle-like fortress was being built on their vast 35-acre estate.

The more Bob gave, however, the more Amy wanted.

"That's narcissism," Phelps said. "They believe they deserve more than what they've been given in life and they're going to take it."

Amy took the opportunity to get more from Bob when he hired her to manage the company's money. Not feeling confident in his own ability to manage the funds and not wanting to hire outside, Bob mistakenly handed over the financial reigns to his wife.

"He didn't really have a reason not to trust her," Scott said. "At least not at that point. He wanted to focus on the work side of things and hated crunching numbers. He had a simple business that he expanded and expanded beyond his expectations. But Amy saw the books, did the taxes and the dollar signs raged in her head. He had given her everything and she was going to take full advantage."

"Amy sees all the money that the business has to pay," Phelps said. "By law, the IRS."

So she began to see the possibilities.

"Write a check to the IRS," Phelps said. "Put it in the books. Bob would see it in the books. But she would never send the check to the IRS. Instead, she would withdraw that money herself and put it somewhere."

Amy would steal more than $100,000 from Bob's corporate account for starters.

"It is a head scratcher," Scott said. "Because had she just asked, asked for anything, Bob would have broken his back to give it to her. But instead, it became more of a thrill, more of an addiction for her to steal from the company account. She got away with the first time and then she just began doing it over and over and over again."

"There is also a line of thinking that she know Bob was getting ready to leave her. So she began stashing money away to get back at him. Still, she could have collected alimony for the rest of her life."

The IRS would eventually catch wind of the fishy accounting coming from Bosley Roofing.

They would send letters asking for what Bob's company owed but Amy would intercept them. She had set up a post office box in which she had diverted all of the IRS correspondence.

Meanwhile, Bob's roofing business continued to flourish. He obtained several new accounts and thought everything was okay.

"While Bob was climbing the business ladder," Phelps said. "Amy was climbing into his business accounts."

The monster Amy had created only grew with time. She would eventually pilfer over a million dollars.

The IRS then believed Bob was committing tax fraud.

An investigator arrived at the home and was intercepted at the door by Amy. She expressed shock at the accusation that Bob was guilty of tax evasion.

They informed Amy that Bob could face prison but that didn't deter Amy from continuing to siphon funds out.

"No one's gonna find out," Phelps said. "I'm gonna take this money and I'm gonna hide it. Why? Because I deserve it. I deserve this!"

The IRS continued to hound the Bosleys but established contact with only Amy. She would again express her surprise to the IRS of her husband's reluctance to contact them.

"She's smarter than the police," Phelps said. "They're never going to figure her out. That's what she's thinking in her mind."

On one occasion, the IRS phoned the Bosley residence and Amy pretended she was Bob, deepening her voice.

"She sounded like Kermit the Frog," Phelps said.

The IRS fell for it. Amy, posing as her husband, agreed to meet with them the following day.

"Her mind raced with options," Scott said. "He would have found out about her stealing and God knows what actions he would have taken. People have gotten divorced for a lot less."

Amy could not let that meeting take place. Her monster had gotten too big. Bob would rake her over the coals in a divorce proceeding.

There was only one way out now.

She got out of bed and looked down at her sleeping husband. Reaching into her purse on the bedside table, she took out a gun.

Still, Amy hesitated as she pointed the gun at her husband's back. Her heart raced.

She could do it.

All she had to do was squeeze...

Amy fired three shots into Bob.

Still alive, her husband floundered out of the bed. He tried to wrest the gun out of her hands.

Weakened from the gunshots, Bob's grip failed him. Amy wrested the gun away and shot him again.

Bob Bosley fell to his knees.

"This was a war between the two that she won," Phelps said. "Amy completes the job by firing six shots into the man she married."

The children didn't know what to do. Their daughter turned off her lights and hid under her covers. Their son did the same.

"Stay in your room!" Amy cried out.

"Two kids are obviously awake in the next room," Phelps said. "Scared. Hugging their pillows. Shaking. Now she's gotta cover her tracks."

Amy picked up the phone and dialed the police.

"Someone is breaking into my house and he's fighting with my husband," Amy screamed into the phone. "I don't know what to do."

Then she pretended to be talking to the intruder.

"'No, you can't go up there! It's my kids!'"

Amy hung up the phone and ran outside. She took an ax and smashed in one of the back windows.

"She had the bright idea of making it look like a robbery," Scott said. "She begins rummaging through the house, opening drawers and tossing items on the floor."

Then the 911 operator would call back...

911: Hello? Ma'am?

Amy: Yes?

911: Alright, is he in the house now?

Amy: He just left but he shot my husband. Oh my God, he shot my husband!

911: He shot your husband?

Amy: Yes! Oh my God!

The police arrived at the home moments later. The patrolman sprinted past Amy and came upon the murder scene.

Bob Bosley's body lay on the floor, filled with bullet holes.

The police were suspicious right off the bat. They thought the scene reeked overkill as thieves would most likely not kill Bob and then turn around and destroy the place.

The area was cordoned off in search of the "intruder". The police brought in sniffer dogs but failed to find anything of note. Helicopters were brought in to search the area, a heavily wooded region but like the dogs, searchers came up with nothing.

But the news of an intruder breaking into a home and killing Bosley hit the news.

Children were kept home from school as it was believed that a maniac was on the loose.

"I can't believe what's happened," Bobby Wahoff said, a neighbor of the Bosleys. "Bob was the nicest guy you could find. He would give you the shirt off his back if he had to."

"She caused a panic in the community by saying that an intruder had broken into her house and shot her husband," Hannah said.

Amy would then tell police that she saw the intruder standing by the bed. The man shot her husband despite her attempts to stop him. She stated that the man pushed her away and scratched her chest. She described the man as "a white guy, in his thirties, very tall with a pointed, mean looking face."

"We believe that a white male suspect entered the Bosley cabin through the back door which was broken," police chief Keith Hill said as he addressed the media the day after the murder. "The strange thing is that nothing appears to be missing and no gun or shell casings have been found. We have no motive at this time and no explanation as to why Bob Bosley was killed."

Amy then took the podium, fighting back tears.

"We have every faith in the police department and the investigation to find this killer," Amy said. "We are helping the authorities in every way we can. Unfortunately, as of now all I can remember is that I woke up and was on the floor. I heard shots and I saw a man leave the house."

"Her story didn't add up from the beginning," Hannah said. "There were no footprints in the home. No one saw anyone suspicious in the area despite a massive search."

Amy also failed to impress police detectives during her questioning after the murder. She told police of instances where Bob would leave her and the kids alone for days at a time, partying up at Lake Cumberland with other women.

"The police felt that her behavior during questioning didn't feel right," Scott said. "She kept crying out, like a bad actress. But no tears were forming in her eyes. There were no streaks of mascara running down her face."

AN AMATEUR KILLER

Amy's sloppiness would get the best of her. She ransacked the home without rhyme or reason and no prints were left behind except her own.

"It looked like a made for TV crime scene," Phelps said. "The cabinets under the sink are open. There's nothing under a sink that is of any value to a thief. As cops begin to scour through the house they find two bullet casings near Bob's body. They find more shell casings. Where? In the washing machine. Now, why would a thief leave shell casings in a washing machine?"

Police would later discover that the Bosleys were having problems in their marriage. Bob, despite the displaying the exterior of a Christian philanthropist in the community, started to spend his weekends on his boat on Lake Cumberland. He would hold parties in which the majority of his guests were women.

Friends of Bob would state that he would be on the lake for days at a time, refusing to tell Amy what he was doing and who he was doing it with.

Detectives began questioning Amy about the rumors they heard about their "open" marriage."

Amy said that Bob "kept secrets" from her and would be gone for days at a time.

"He liked to have a lot of women and have big parties on his boat," prosecuting attorney Michelle Snodgrass said. Police

would track down and uncover incriminating evidence of Bob with other women. They confirmed at least one affair but remained firm that the bigger secret was Amy's embezzlement of Bob's company funds.

Prosecutors would later state that she was destroying his business to "get even with him for being unfaithful."

"Amy once told me that if Bob was ever unfaithful to her or left her she would shoot him," Debbie Webb, Bob's sister said. "Shoot him in his sleep. I didn't take this seriously but it lingered in the back of my mind."'

"The police now have a motive," Scott said. "It became clear to them that Amy was simply covering her tracks. She didn't think the murder through any more than she thought through the theft of Bob's money."

MORE EVIDENCE NEEDED

The police had a motive but they did not have enough physical evidence to convict Amy.

Investigators would find a suicide letter in the home, signed by Bob Bosley. Amy would tell police that her husband had written it as a joke.

The police were split in their assessment of what the letter meant. Some thought that Bob was ready to commit suicide. Others thought that the letter sounded as if he was getting ready to abandon his family. The letter was addressed to Amy and the two children.

The district attorney, however, said that the letter wasn't written by Bob Bosley at all.

All fingers pointed at Amy.

"I loved Bob," Amy said during an interrogation session with detectives. "Despite any problems we had. We didn't have a perfect marriage -who does? - but he was the father of my children and I had no reason to shoot him."

The police didn't buy the story. Three days later, after much deliberation, they arrested and charged Amy with murder.

The prosecution would reveal that during a police search of the cabin they had found Amy's purse hidden in the back of one of the cupboards. Inside was a Glock handgun that her husband owned.

Her defense attorney, Jim Morgan, stated that there was no evidence that the Glock was the weapon used to kill Bob.

"There were no witnesses," Morgan said. "No DNA evidence and the possibility of another killer can't be ruled out because Bob Bosley had made many enemies through his business dealings."

The prosecution, however, used interviews of the children to seal Amy's guilt.

"She had spiked the kids' drink so they would sleep through this," Hannah said. "But I don't know how anyone could sleep through a 9mm gun being fired multiple times. And the children didn't."

The children would reveal to police that they heard a "loud bang" several times before hearing the glass smash. Then they heard things being thrown around.

"Both children were interviewed separately," Scott said. "They were both adamant that they heard the glass breaking downstairs after they heard the gunshots. This affirmed to the police that Amy had staged the crime. They just had to break her down."

Amy finally cracked when her children's testimony is revealed. The prosecution offered a plea bargain of twenty years and she accepted.

Amy's attorney would later state that she took the deal because she didn't want her children to testify.

The Bosley family argued otherwise, stating that it was the family's wish for the prosecution to push for the plea deal.

"Amy didn't care if those kids were on the stand," James Bosley said. "She doesn't even care about them today. She could care less about them kids. She's not even a mother in my eyes."

"She kept up a charade for several years," Scott said. "She just wanted money from Bob. She married him for the money and would kill him for it."

Amy was sentenced to twenty years in prison but would refuse to disclose what she did with the money.

The Bosley family was livid but were given an opportunity to confront the woman who killed Bob.

"You have no respect for life," Bob's brother James said. "You are a liar and a fake.

"Did he yell out for you to stop?" Debra Webb, Bob's brother asked. "We'll never know."

"I didn't get to see my son," Audrey Bosley, Bob's mother read from a letter. "I didn't get to tell him goodbye."

Amy would look down on the floor during the confrontation. She would sob intermittently.

"You can walk out of jail," James Bosley, Bob's brother said. "Dig up the loot we believe you stole from my brother's business and live the rest of your life in luxury. All we hope is that every night you see the face of my brother and the tear-stained faces of your children who have been turned into orphans and who saw horrors that will stay with them for the rest of their lives."

"Just look ahead maybe," Phelps said. "We can see her in the middle of the night some night, with a flashlight and a shovel, all by herself, looking around digging in that hole, coming up with that shoebox full of money and just laughing all the way to the bank."

Amy Bosley becomes eligible for parole in 2020.

DRUG CRAZED KILLER : THE TRUE STORY OF ROSIE ALFARO

137

ELIZABETH MARKS

Maria del Rosio Alfaro, better known to the media a Rosie Alfaro, is the first woman to be sentenced to death in Orange County. Her story is a tragic one, set in a town nearby Disneyland in Anaheim, California. By the time that Rosie was thirteen, she was heavily into drugs and considered by many to be an addict. At this age, Rosie was often doing fifty speedballs a day for weeks at a time, a speedball being a mixture of heroin and cocaine. Regular doses of this highly addictive cocktail were just the first steps along a dark path, and in grade seven she dropped out of school. By the time that Rosie was fourteen years old, she had become a prostitute. Despite efforts from her mother to get her back on track, a tormented and abused past pushed her forward on her path of self-destruction

At the witness stand in a court case only a few years after this point in her life, an old friend of Rosie's Tamara Benedict testified that at that time they both often slept with drug dealers for money so that they could buy drugs. Sometimes just receive their payment in narcotics directly. Benedict claimed "we had no jobs at all" and "sometimes we would steal from stores or get someone to steal for us." By the time that Rosie was fifteen, she was a single mother. At 18, she was a mother of two and pregnant with twins. It is also at this age that she committed the murder that would ruin her life.

When Rosie had been pregnant with her second child, she had spent some time living at the Wallace residence, the family of one of her friends from school. The Wallace's had three girls, Amber, April, and Autumn. Rosie was friends with April Wallace and was taking shelter at their house during one of the most difficult periods of her life. After her time living with the family, she got back into drugs, became distant, and had very little contact. The only time that she would have any association with the family would be when she was offered a lift somewhere.

A year later, when Rosie had had the baby and was pregnant with the twins, she was living with a relative of the father from her most recent pregnancy. This house was three blocks away from the Wallace residence. Rosie was on another drug binge at the time and had her first hit at eleven in the morning. By 2 PM she was getting desperate for another fix. She began to think about how she could acquire the money for more drugs. She mentioned to the men that she was with, the three of them looking after her oldest child, that she had an old video camera that she had left at the Wallace residence. She asked them to drive her to the residence so that she could retrieve it, and that she would gladly trade this camera in for cash so that they could all get another hit. The two men, Rosie, and her eldest boy who was only fourteen months old at the time drove to the Wallace residence. Rosie got out by herself to go and knock at the door, and the two men stood outside of the car with the baby. Rosie has made different testimonies in her time, both claiming that she didn't know that nine-year-old Autumn Wallace would be home and that she did realize. Whichever of these is true, Rosie knocked on the front door and

Autumn answered. Based on her testimonies, it is more likely that she was expecting Autumn to be home so that somebody would enable her to get inside of the house.

Autumn's school had had an 'early day' that afternoon, and they had let the children leave at 2:35PM. Her mother wasn't due home from work until after five, and neither of her sisters were home. Rosie asked if she would be able to use their bathroom to fix her hair and freshen herself up. Autumn, who remembered Rosie from the time that she spent living with the family, didn't hesitate to let her in. Before Rosie had knocked at the door, Autumn had been cutting out paper dolls. She went back to her task in the living room. On her way to the bathroom, Rosie went to the kitchen and picked up a knife. In the bathroom, she created a ruse to trick Autumn. She claimed that she needed assistance with an eyelash curler, and asked Autumn to come into the bathroom to help her. When Autumn entered the bathroom, Rosie grabbed her. "That's when I did it," Alfaro told the investigators. "I stabbed her . . . 'cause she knew who I was," Rosie claims that Autumn made no sound when she was attacked and that nobody else was involved. "I was too high; I just remember her looking at me," Alfaro when she was interviewed at Orange County Jail. "Before, sometimes at night, the day would come back, and I'd block that out. Now I think about it more and more, because blocking is not working." Alfaro attacked Autumn with such ferocity that she died on the spot.

In all of Rosie's later testimonies, she claims that she was forced to stab the girl by one of the men who had accompanied her. She also claims that she stabbed Autumn several times, but that she did not finish the deed. Whether Rosie acted alone or with this man who she still refuses to identify, Autumn Wallace was stabbed fifty-seven times in her face, chest, and back. After this time, Rosie claims that she and the man went around the house stealing a few items. They took a portable TV, a typewriter, a telephone and a Nintendo set. Later on, they sold these items for a mere $300. As Rosie began to come down off her high, she realized the severity of the things that she had done and the guilt began to set in. She began to panic, and it was then that she made plans for her escape.

At 5:15 PM, April Wallace returned home. She found the door unlocked and the house in a mess. She called out to Autumn but got no response. She immediately ran to the house across the street for safety where she could wait for her mother to come home. Linda Wallace, the girls' mother, arrived home at 5:40 PM. She was told that her house had been burgled and that Autumn was missing. Believing that her girl might be hiding, she went inside the house to search for the youngest daughter and found her in the back bathroom in a pool of blood. Neighbors told Linda that they had seen a brownish Monte Carlo parked outside of the Wallace house and that two men were standing outside of the car. One of them was holding a small child. Police fingerprinted the house and found prints that matched

Alfaro's. They brought Rosie in for questioning, and she denied any involvement in the murder, or that she has been near the house at all. As they didn't have any further evidence or a witness that could identify her having been at the house, Rosie was let go.

At some point after the murder, Rosie asked one of her friends if she could leave a bag full of clothing outside of their house. She had made plans to leave for Mexico the next day, and wanted this bag to be easily accessible. However, Rosie never showed up. Investigators found out about the bag and inside they found a pair of Alfaro's tennis shoes and a pair of April Wallace's boots stolen from the house. They put out a warrant of arrest for Alfaro, and brought her in for questioning again. It was at this point that Alfaro began to realize that she wouldn't get away with the crime, and that she would have to be more cooperative with the police.

Alfaro identified one of the men that she had been with as Antonio Reynoso, being the man who stayed in the car with her son. Antonio had been released from prison the previous day. He had agreed to share his drugs with Rosie is she was happy to share her needle. The other man, who Rosie claims was active in the killing of Autumn Wallace, she has persistently refused to identify over the years, and only refers to by the name of Beto. Alfaro has said several times in court that she is not able to identify this man for the police as she fears for the safety of her children and her partner. Even if the face of the death penalty, Rosie did not reveal the identity of this man, and he still remains a mystery. Some members of the court have claimed that they feel the story of Beto is a fabrication, and that Rosie committed the crime by herself. However, there is some evidence to suggest that her claims might be true. Not only did neighbors see the two men out the front of the house, but a footprint in the bathroom that was initially thought to belong to Rosie was found to not match the shoes that she had been wearing. While all of the prints had initially been assumed to be Alfaro's, criminologist Marc Taylor found that there was also another set of prints both inside and outside of the house. This gives some credibility to Alfaro's story, but her unwillingness to identify the man means that she is taking the full consequences for the situation alone. Alfaro claims that when Beto saw that Autumn was home, he became enraged and put a knife to Rosie's back. He threatened to stab her if she wasn't going to stab Autumn. Rosie admits to stabbing Autumn several times, but maintains that Beto was the one who did the majority of the stabbing and caused Autumn's death. "If I wasn't so scared my family would get hurt, I'd tell the truth, but I just can't," she said in court. Even though it means that she is potentially getting the death sentence for a crime that she didn't solely commit, she remains silent on this issue in order to protect her family.

As Rosie plans to die with the identity of Beto, it is likely that this person will never be brought to justice and remains at large. Rosie initially claimed that the man was a friend of her father's, and that his name was Miguel. Later she claimed that this was not true and that the man who she would only name as Beto had a woman's name tattooed on the side of his neck. Alfaro identified a photo of the man. Orange County investigator Robert Harper identified the likely identity of this man to be Robert Frias Gonzalez, but Rosie gave no confirmation of this suspicion. It was later revealed the that tattoo on the side of his man's neck was actually a butterfly, but due to Rosie's state of mind and drug abuse her claims have not been judged as entirely false. It is impossible to say whether Rosie was identifying a photograph just to appease the police, and that this explains the difference between the tattoos, whether she was in such a state of mind that she couldn't remember the tattoo correctly, or whether the man had any identifiable tattoos done over with larger and darker designs to hide what was underneath. The fact that there is a discrepancy between the tattoos certainly doesn't factor this final consideration. Perhaps if his tattoo was the name is a lost loved one, he marked it with a butterfly to keep his display of respect? A deputy sheriff at the Orange County jail testified that he had seen a man similar to the one that Rosie had identified in the picture getting into a blue Camaro outside of the Orange County jail. From the evidence, it would certainly seem that another person was present at the residence and may have had involvement in the murder of Autumn Wallace, but without Alfaro's testimony on this matter nothing more can be pursued.

In the courtroom Alfaro, wearing a floral blouse and blue stretch pants, cried throughout Tamara Benedict's testimony and also those of her childhood friends, her boyfriend

Manuel Cueva, and her mother Silvia Melendez Alfaro. When Cueva described the visits of Alfaro's children to the County jail as Rosie awaited trial, she openly sobbed. Sylvia Alfaro made every attempt possible to try to create some sympathy and understanding for Rosie, painting an image of the horrific childhood that she had suffered through. Sylvia testified that her husband was a dreadful alcoholic who regularly hit her and Rosie in front of the other children in the family. He would also often throw the whole family out of the house when he was in a drunken rage. Alfaro's mother discussed Rosie's early drug use and how she seemed totally unable to quit her habits, constantly seeking to get some distance from the real world. When Rosie was pregnant with her first child at the age of fourteen, her father left home and abandoned the family. Sylvia claimed that Rosie completely lost control of her drug addiction at the age of fifteen. "She wore heavy makeup, black clothes and was always dirty. She didn't care how she looked." From this point until when Rosie attacked Autumn, she was in an almost constant state of pregnancy. With no other way to support her habit, she slept with her dealers and attempted to look after her children as best she could.

A mental health expert, Dr. Consuelo Edwards, was the first one that Rosie had told about Beto. It was Edwards that recommended that she should speak about Beto in court, and he also came forward to defend her with his testimony. From his interactions with Rosie, Edwards deemed that her intellectual functioning was 'borderline' and that he feels that she has a serious learning disability. He didn't argue that he felt this excused any of her behavior, but that it should be something to factor when the jury are arriving at their decision. He tested Rosie as having an IQ of 78, and testified that her intellectual issues were made worse by the traumatic experiences that she had gone through as a child. In reaction to these claims, the prosecutor called forth several employees at the Orange County jail who testified to Rosie's poor behavior in jail. These employees also claimed that they had heard Rosie saying "I'm a frustrated person who takes things out on people, and have to learn to live with that," and "I'm not going to be able to do this again. I'm no actor. I'm going to be cold this time. I just want to get this over with." It is not certain whether this was a move to try to paint Rosie as an inherently bad or disturbed person, as this claims as nothing to do with her capacity intellectually. Perhaps they were making the argument that Rosie's lack of intellectual giftedness mean that she wasn't able to reflect on her own behavior and that way that she treated others. However these testimonies were intended, they painted Rosie as incredibly difficult to deal with and as somebody who lashes out with quick and ill-thought-through responses.

The first jury that assessed the case was on 14th July 1992. The judge for this case claimed that her crime was the most "senseless, brutal, vicious, and callous killing" that he had ever known. The jury was a deadlock with 10:2 in favor of Rosie receiving the death penalty, meaning that this was not enough to hand down the sentence. A deadlock means that the required amounts of votes was not reached, and in order to place a person on Death Row every member of the jury needed to agree that this was the proper course of action according to the evidence that they had viewed during the case. When Rosie was reflecting on this outcome and how close she had come to being sentenced to death, she claimed that "I do think that someone has to pay for what happened to that poor little girl, and that's me," she said. "But I can't help thinking how my life stopped, ended, at 18, and that I have no future, and all that is because of drugs." In many ways, Alfaro has distanced herself not only from the person that she was when she committed the crime, but the person who engaged in the type of lifestyle that she did before that. As she awaited her next trial date, she claimed that she would spend all day trying not to think about how likely it was that she would be sentenced to death and instead thought about the ways in which drugs had wasted her life.

Then in 2007, another court hearing was held where the jury placed forward the unanimous decision for the death sentence. During this trial, Rosie claimed that she was constantly haunted by her actions. She read out a letter that she had written to Autumn. "I have a picture of you in my Bible, and every time I open it, I see your innocent face and I think of my boys and what I would do if something were ever to happen to them. . . . So please know that I am deeply and truly sorry, Autumn, and I will pay for the rest of my life for what happened." Nobody can be sure whether this was an attempt to show remorse and soften the approach of the jury or whether Alfaro simply felt the need to be able to express these feelings in a more public context than she was capable of in jail. Perhaps Alfaro wanted for the Wallace family to hear that she was experiencing remorse over the issue, and that she was making a genuine attempt to comprehend and suffer for the things that she had done. When the sentence was handed down, Deputy Dist. Atty. Charles J. Middleton described the jury's decision as "justified" and claims that he knew the outcome based on the amount of time that the jury took considering the evidence, saying "I was sure it was a death verdict because I could not imagine 12 people agreeing that soon that this kind of a crime should not get a death sentence." These jury members deliberated for just over two days before they released their unanimous recommendation. When the sentence was handed down, it was met with clapping and cheering from the Wallace family and gasps and shock from the Alfaros and their supporters. Alfaro later claimed: "I know it's hard for the Wallaces to forgive me, and I don't ask for their forgiveness," Alfaro said. "If it had been one of my kids that was killed—I'm a mother too—I'd probably do the same thing: celebrate." William M. Monroe, who was Alfaro's attorney, quoted Alfaro as saying "I can't believe this. It can't happen to me. . . . Why did they (jurors) do this?" after the sentence was brought down. Monroe also made some emotional claims, seemingly unable to believe that Alfaro was truly going to be placed on Death Row. "I'm probably as shocked by the verdict as Rosie Alfaro is," Monroe said outside the courtroom. "I still contend that this crime was committed by a person with an abandoned and malignant heart, and Rosie Alfaro is not (such) a person." Monroe mentioned that "I feel terrible, absolutely terrible for what happened to Autumn Wallace, but this little girl, this young woman-child, does not deserve" and that he would file an appeal. After the verdict was served, photographers and cameramen were crowded around the courthouse hoping to catch a glimpse of the grief-ridden Alfaro. Alfaro supporters shielded their faces and turned their backs in an attempt to avoid the media. "Nobody wants to talk right now. We have no words," said a friend of the defendant. As with all cases, there was a lot of initial hype but it slowly died down. Now, when searching about the Alfaro case, there is rarely a recent article that will give any updates or further information on the matter. Rosie is simply on Death Row awaiting her visit to the gas chamber as her sons continue to grow up without her presence.

Much of the coverage around the case has regarded the behavior and quotes of the two mothers in the courtroom: Linda Wallace the mother of the deceased Autumn who claimed to fight for justice for her daughter's death, and Sylvia Alfaro who was fighting for the life of her own daughter. Linda Wallace made an emotional plea to the courtroom, claiming that during the trial her daughter has only been known as a young victim stabbed to death by somebody that she trusted. The grieving mother wanted everybody to know what Autumn was really like, and that was she so much more than the court case had reduced her to. She spoke about her blonde hair and brown eyes, and that she was an A student who loved swimming and fishing. She was incredibly creative, and wanted to be an artist when she grew up. Of Rosie, Linda claimed that what she did is horrible and that she will "never forgive or forget her." To Sylvia Alfaro, Linda said that she really felt for her because she knows what it feels like to lose a daughter.

Sylvia Alfaro was similarly trying to expand the way that the people in court were viewing her daughter, saying that "The first time that I came here, I felt like I was sitting in the electric chair," she cried. "I beg you, please forgive my daughter and please forgive what she did," Sylvia claimed that Rosie's issues with drugs had gotten a lot worse after the birth of her daughter's first son Daniel, and that she had enrolled her daughter in several drug programs in an attempt to beat her habits. Unfortunately, she always went back to her old ways after a few months. However, Sylvia maintains that while Rosie was pregnant she usually managed to control her drug addiction. This does not align with the information that was presented before the court on the day of Autumn Wallace's murder. This particular binge might well have been an isolated event or even an extended period of drug usage, but in either case, it would have been difficult for the jury to believe that Rosie was not a drug user during pregnancies when the entire case revolved around her desperation for another hit. Sylia had even gone so far as to sent her daughter to Mexico to live with her grandmother in the hope that this distance and change of environment would help her to get away from the complicated lifestyle around drugs, but this change in location didn't make any difference. She ended up coming back home when her grandmother was not able to cope with her behavior, and she fell into the same patterns.

Monroe, the attorney, attempted to raise some sympathy for Rosie regarding her troubled past and attempted to make the case that she should be sent to prison instead of the gas chamber. He made this assertion based on her addiction to drugs and her being the mother of four young boys. He claimed that the jury made a mistake in their recommendation, and he also introduced the notion of race. Monroe claimed that the mainly white jury could not possibly understand what it was to grow up in a household like Rosie had, and that they could not "empathize, understand or relate" to Latino women trapped in the drug world. While it might be true that somebody in a very different demographic cannot fully understand the life of somebody who has endured so much pain, the purpose of a jury is to find a random sampling of people who can determine what they feel is just action and what behavior should be acceptable in our society. Regardless of Alfaro's abuse in her childhood and early teens, the murder of a nine-year-old girl is not something that the jury considered as acceptable behavior.

Linda Wallace and her daughters had been traveling from their new homes in Lake Havasu , Arizona, the girls both having married and started their own families. April Nunez and Amber Szabo had been traveling in support of their deceased sister and trying to come to terms with her loss. In one interview, their mother Linda claimed that "You would think after all this time, you would get over it, but you don't." When asked how she endured through a trial, two penalty hearings, and a fifteen-year wait for the appellate review, Linda claimed that "I was doing it for Autumn." Later she also claimed that "it's the only thing I can do for her," the mom said, "I need to be there to represent her because she can't do it. I go to be with my daughter." Linda Wallace has also confided in several interviews how she feels outside of the court. "The hardest thing for me is to see people now who are Autumn's age," she said. "Not being able to see her grow up, that's what bothers me the most. She would be 26 years old now. She could be married. She could have kids. That's what I think about." Linda says that she has spent the years waiting for justice, and not spending her time or energy thinking about Alfaro. "I know she is in a bad place," Wallace says. "I know she will never see the light of day. I am fine with it." Linda also commented that Alfaro hasn't had much of a life since her arrest: "she just exists," the mother said. "It wouldn't be any life I would want." While the Wallace mother was one of the members of the family who was clapping when the sentence was passed down and has also been somebody to proclaim often and loudly that her daughter needs justice, she has also stated that she doesn't feel the need for Alfaro to be executed. In some ways, this might be an attempt to show a soft side to the media as in many of her interviews she claims that she waited fifteen years for the sentence to be handed down, when Alfaro had been imprisoned for that entire duration. This suggests that, in some way, Linda Wallace did feel that it was necessary for Rosie to be put on Death Row to properly avenge Autumn's death.

April and Amber have expressed similar long-lasting hatred of Rosie. "We get nothing," Zabo said. "And she gets all of these things. It makes me mad. ... I just want to see her be put to death, and I want to see it faster than it is taking." When April was asked if she would travel to San Quentin Prison to watch Alfaro get executed, she said "Oh yes, I would go to watch her die, without a doubt. I would do it myself if they'd let me." Linda Wallace was also asked in the same interview, she responded "I am not that much for that," she said. "If she is put to death, then another mother loses her child. I know what it feels like to lose a child." But her other interactions with the media suggest that Rosie getting the death penalty gave her some sense of relief and faith in the system.

The judge, Middleton, claimed that Monroe did not give any credence to Monroe's claims of racial misconception, and asserted that the jury had made their decision purely based on facts. He went on to say that she made her own choices in life and that Rosie cannot blame her action on others no matter how poor her treatment as a child and young adult had been. He also put forward the opinion that based on the evidence in court he did not believe that Rosie Alfaro was capable of looking after her children. Alfaro was convicted of first-degree murder with special circumstances, the circumstances being that the murder offered during the felonies of Burglary and Robbery. Alfaro joined two other women on Death Row, Maureen McDermott and Cynthia Lynn Coffman. McDermott was a Los Angeles registered nurse who was convicted in 1990 of hiring a co-worker to murder her roommate. It was found that Maureen planned to collect on a $100 00 mortgage insurance policy. Coffman was convicted in 1986 of the kidnapping and murder of a woman in San Bernardino. Capital punishment was restored in California in 1978, and these are the only three women to receive the death penalty in that time.

Since she was handed down the death sentence, Alfaro says that she spends her time thinking about how misguided her drug addled youth was, what happened to Autumn, and the days when her children will be old enough to know what she did. "God, I hate to think of the future, because there's not a future for me and my kids," she said. "It's going to be up to (them) if they still want to call me mom when they find out. I know they're going to find out sooner or later, and I'm scared of what they're going to decide." Alfaro is now 44 years old and still on Death Row with his four children still being cared for by boyfriend Cueva. She will not get to see them grow up, and may not feel that she deserves to give them any guidance in doing so. In many ways, she is now waiting for death as she no longer has a functional life. Waiting for the nightmare to be over do that she no longer has to block out the deeds of her past.

A SAVAGE BITCH : THE TRUE STORY OF IRENE MASLIN

155

ANNE MASON

IRENE MASLIN

Despite being a bit rough around the edges, many of the townspeople residing in the rural countryside of Mirboo North in Victoria, Australia would vouch for 28-year-old motorcycle enthusiast Paul Snabel. It was true that the young man had a penchant for reckless driving. heavy drinking, and frequent drug use; however, those that knew him best saw straight through his bad boy facade. He was often described as openly affectionate and he cared deeply for his family. People enjoyed being around Paul, despite his flaws. In fact, Paul's magnetic personality made him the sort of man with plenty of friends and very few enemies.

When Paul disappeared suddenly after attending a party at the home of Donna Randall in November 1989, his flatmate was not immediately concerned for his well being. After binging on a cocktail of drugs and alcohol, Snabel would sometimes be prone to taking off on impromptu joyrides across the open roads. Even after a week or so without any contact, loved ones did not suspect that Paul could have possibly been the victim of a violent crime. Instead, people assumed that he had finally succumbed to his vices. Suspecting that he may have careened off of a steep cliff in a drunken stupor, local authorities proceeded to conduct an extensive search along Victoria's highways.

Instead of recovering a body, police were surprised to find pieces of Snabel's most prized possession – a red and white striped Yamaha motorcycle – disassembled across several garbage dumps and dams. In the coming weeks, the abandoned pieces would prove to be the first of many clues pointing to a stunning conspiracy revolved around love lost and a callous, brutal murder, unlike anything the area had experienced before or since.

* * *

Police first began to seriously suspect foul play upon receiving a report from a farmer who had stumbled upon a lone bike engine. Though authorities were sure that the engine was in fact consistent with the model whose scattered parts were surfacing across the countryside, it became evident upon closer investigation that someone had attempted to file off the vehicle's serial number. Puzzled, investigators had little choice but to retrace Paul's steps – which quickly led them to Donna Randall and her sister, Karen.

The Randall sisters were no strangers to Snabel; in fact, it quickly became apparent that Karen and Paul had been involved in a volatile relationship for a number of years. At the time of his disappearance, the two were separated; Paul's amphetamine use was beginning to spiral out of control, and after a series of physical confrontations, she sought a clean break. However, Snabel was less than thrilled to leave behind Randall. When Karen and her young son moved to a neighboring town in an attempt to escape the toxic environment, Paul tracked down Randall's child and followed him home from school. Upon discovering Karen's new address, he left an intimidating note on the front of her door, causing her a great deal of anxiety and concern.

Nevertheless, the sisters confirmed that Paul had in fact recently attended a house party at Donna's residence despite the troubling history he shared with Karen. Afterward, he had followed the sisters back to mutual friend Rhona Heaney's home. However, the Randall sisters insisted that they had grown tired of his drunken, unruly behavior and had ordered him to leave. Though the authorities were convinced of the women's innocence in the disappearance, they decided to visit Rhona Heaney in hopes of tracking down some significant leads. Once there, Rhona corroborated the story Donna and Karen had provided; the only additional piece of information she was able to provide concerned dropping her children off at the home of Irene Maslin prior to Snabel's arrival.

Feeling that their line of questioning wasn't leading anywhere meaningful, investigators began to instead focus their attention on the recovered bike parts. By the time they had begun questioning suspects, they had recovered enough pieces to almost completely reassemble the bike to its original state. As they began to place the evidence together, they noticed a very peculiar detail; the wiring of the motorcycle had been found neatly coiled and carefully placed in individual plastic bags. As it turned out, those plastic bags were uniquely designed for the state electricity commission. Upon contacting the commission, it was revealed that the bags were not readily available to the general public. After searching through a list of employees and comparing it with the names of individuals involved in the investigation, it was discovered that Irene Maslin's husband, Jano, was an electrician with the state. Having finally found a potential suspect – however tenuous their lead may have been – the police eagerly began to investigate.

* * *

On the surface, Irene Maslin appeared to be nothing more than a typical housewife. After immigrating from Holland as a small child in 1954, she attended high school locally, worked on a farm, and eventually took on a position as a nursing aide in a nearby hospital. After giving birth to a son with a previous husband, Irene met Jano at a Rotary Club meeting and quickly fell in love. Like many of the women in her small town, she enjoyed domestic activities such as cooking and gardening. Although she did not have any children with Jano, she was a well-known maternal figure in the community and frequently served as a "carekeeper". She has a reputation for knitting jumpers and accessories for expectant mothers and newborns. Irene even held an excellent rapport with the local church. With no history of prior arrests, investigators were skeptical that a trip to the Maslin household would yield any answers to the mysterious departure of Paul Snabel.

Playing the part of an average, law-abiding couple, both Jano and Irene were initially cooperative and welcomed the inquisitive investigators to search their home as they pleased. Nothing immediately stood out as suspicious. However, when they reached the garage, they found plastic bags identical to the ones found at the dump as well as several electrical cords neatly coiled in a fashion similar to the wiring recovered from the Yamaha. Lodged in the cracks of the concrete floor, flecks of red paint consistent with that of the motorbike were discovered. Also recovered inside of the garage was a used a metal file, which was covered with remnants of the same red paint.

As evidence began leaving their home for further examination, the Maslin's attitude towards the police quickly became hostile. In contrast to their initial friendliness, Jano Maslin ultimately shooed away the authorities and, on behalf of his wife, insisted that the two had no statement to provide concerning the crime. The next time investigators returned to the Maslin residence, they discovered that the married couple had packed their belongings and left town without any indicator of when they might return. Neighbors asserted that the Maslin's had gone on a Christmas vacation, although it quickly became clear that no one had an idea of where exactly they had traveled to for the holidays.

As the search for the Maslin's began, a very different portrait of Irene was painted by neighbors and friends. The townspeople of Mirboo North, frightened of her "intimidating aura", were hesitant to cross the seemingly harmless woman. The amiable, kind-hearted persona she had presented began to disintegrate as anecdotes recounting her domineering personality and aggressive behavior began to emerge. On one occasion, it was reported that Irene had hired "big blokes" to beat a man that tried her patience. Others confessed that Maslin was a frequent drug trafficker that ran with industry "heavy hitters". According to those individuals, she openly dealt amphetamines and imported kilos of marijuana from New South Wales. Though the line between rumor and reality was hazy at best, one thing became evident; the situation that the police had stumbled into was much more dangerous than they could have initially anticipated.

* * *

Days passed without a trace of Jano or Irene Maslin. Attention shifted back to Karen Randall, who had checked herself into a local hospital because of her fragile emotional state. When questioned a second time by authorities, she broke down in tears and redacted the original statement she had provided regarding Paul's disappearance. Karen then admitted that Irene had been at Rhona's house on the day of the disappearance, directly contradicting Maslin's previous statements claiming that she had never met Snabel. Several days later, Donna Randall came forward to admit that her prior testimony had been inaccurate as well. Following the hospitalization, Irene and Rhona had begun to suspect that that Karen might be talking to authorities. In an attempt to intimidate the Randall sisters, Heaney and Maslin had fetched Donna in the dead of night and ordered her to keep her sister quiet. Insinuating that their lives may be in danger if they failed to oblige, Donna made the decision to cooperate with police in exchange for safety from her friends turned tormentors.

Just a few days before Paul's disappearance, the Randall sisters had shared afternoon tea with Rhona and Irene. At that time, Karen confided in her friends her concerns regarding the increasingly unstable affair she shared with Snabel. Disgusted by Snabel's behavior, the women began discussing possible solutions to Karen's recurring relationship issues. When someone suggested in jest that they simply kill the man, Irene Maslin in particular latched onto the idea and refused to let go. The master manipulator then goaded the three women into a sinister murder plot.

Following Donna's party, Karen baited the inebriated Snabel into visiting Rhona Heaney's secluded countryside home with promises of rekindling the bond they once shared. Upon his arrival, he was instead greeted by Irene and Rhona, who coerced him into taking some drugs. The women had assured him that the syringes they offered were filled with speed; however, they failed to mention that the amphetamines were laced with corrosive battery acid. Being fully aware that the concentrated sulfuric acid would quickly wreak havoc on Paul's body and result in a gruesome death, Karen and Donna opted to leave Rhona's home once the substance began flowing through his veins. Though neither sister had witnessed the death or viewed the corpse, they hadn't heard from him following the events at the Heaney household. Several days later, Rhona and Irene mentioned having sold the couch Paul sat on because they were unable to remove the stains he left behind. In addition, Irene had organized and constructed the stories each woman provided to officers upon investigation.

Using the information Donna provided, police continued to pursue the Maslin's with new fervor. With a new lead on the location of their vacation getaway, they anxiously arrived at an address in the sparsely populated countryside. Instead of finding their suspects, authorities were greeted by Ian GIllin, an ex-footballer who happened to be friends with the women in question. When asked about his whereabouts during the time of the disappearance, he immediately admitted that he had been with the Maslin's on the day of the crime. He claimed to have spent the day digging the foundation for a new swimming pool in the backyard, and had only briefly met Paul. That evening, Jano Maslin left the property for several hours, then returned with the red and white Yamaha motorcycle. Ian was then ordered to disassemble the bike, and being a simple man, he helped without much question. Jano and Ian then proceeded to scatter the parts of the motorcycle across several dumps, dams, and bushes nearby. Matching the locations of the recovered Yamaha with the locations Ian Gillin referenced in his testimony, it became clear that he was, in fact, the person behind the destruction of Paul Snabel's bike.

With enough damning evidence in their hands to be sure of the women's involvement in Snabel's disappearance, warrants for the arrests of Irene Maslin and Rhona Heaney were filed. When they eventually returned home after their holiday vacation, they were promptly taken into custody.

The two women were reacting to the circumstances in drastically different ways. On one hand, Irene's attitude upon being taken into the station could best be described as contemptuous. As investigators began asking questions concerning the crime, she remained silent and steady. Her stony face showed no signs of guilt or remorse, though it was clear that she had something to hide. Rhona, on the other hand, was anxious and initially hesitant to confirm or deny the truthfulness of her original statements to police. Without letting much time pass, she came to the conclusion that she could not escape punishment. Unwilling to take all of the blame for the heinous crime, she agreed to provide further details regarding the last moments of Paul Snabel's short life.

* * *

Hours after the initial injection of battery acid, it appeared that the poison was not especially effective; rather than collapsing or writhing in pain, Paul continued about his business and even began riding his motorcycle around Heaney's backyard. Frustrated by their failure, the women were forced plan a different course of action. As Snabel remained completely oblivious to the women's evil intentions, Irene made arrangements for Ian Gillin to be dropped off at Rhona's home. There, the two men met for the first time and shared a drink or two. About a half hour into Ian's visit, Maslin pulled the young man aside and informed him that Paul "had to go". She then handed Gillin a child's metal baseball bat and badgered him into hitting Snabel across the head with it. Although the two barely knew each other, Gillin agreed to it out of fear. Immediately, the blow knocked Paul unconscious; during that time, the women forced another dose of battery acid into his body.

Evidently, that wasn't enough to kill him. As Paul began to moan and groan in pain, Irene began to scream at Ian to continue hitting the severely injured man. Startled, Ian Gillin swung the bat several times, fracturing Snabel's skull and splattering blood across the room. Horrified by his own actions, he became sick and stepped away from the battered, dying man. Rhona, equally horrified by the gruesome turn of events, witnessed Irene finish Paul off once and for all. Incredibly, after sustaining a number of hits to the head, he continued to cling to life and gasp for breath. Irene proceeded to grab a plastic bag, place it over the man's bloodied head, and secure it into place with a rubber band. Together, Rhona and Irene watched as their defenseless victim slowly suffocated.

Once the deed was done, Irene's husband and Ian set to work on disposing of the bike. Meanwhile, Irene and Rhona wrapped the body in a plastic tarp and unceremoniously shoved it into the back seat of their Subaru. The two women then drove deep into the isolated bushlands and dumped the corpse far from the nearest town. They also carefully disposed of all of the incriminating evidence involved in the murder.

As the police followed up on Rhona's account, the mystery finally began to gain some clarity. After tracking down Ian GIllin, he confirmed Heaney's version of events. He added crucial details regarding the intimidation tactics Irene employed; when he initially pulled away from the metal baseball bat, Maslin assured him that Paul would kill Karen unless Ian took initiative and killed him first. When Gillin continued to show reservations about murdering Snabel, Maslin began to imply that Ian might find himself in trouble if he did not do as Irene commanded. Asserting that his actions were a measure of self-defense against Irene's wrath, he had no issues taking responsibility for the crime he had committed.

Forensic teams later lifted the lining of Rhona Heaney's living room carpet and found blood stains soaked deep into the base of the floor. Unfortunately, at the time DNA testing was not readily available, making it impossible to know for sure whether or not the blood found beneath the carpet belonged to Paul. Luckily, DNA proof was not necessary for charging the criminals or discovering the fate of Paul Snabel. Using Rhona's account of where the body was dumped, police uncovered scraps of torn clothing and fragments of a human skeleton in the bush. There, they were lucky enough to recover an intact skull and jawbone; Snabel's dental records matched that of the skeleton, finally providing conclusive evidence for family and friends as to where Paul had disappeared to for so many months

* * *

After a bizarre and tumultuous investigation, prosecutors were finally able to take the case to trial and present their evidence to a stunned jury. Although Karen Randall was the impetus behind the murder, she ultimately only received two years in prison for her involvement in the plot to kill her former lover. Her sister, Donna, was awarded an identical sentence. Ian Gillin was charged and found guilty of manslaughter. He served three years behind bars before earning his freedom. The court was much less lenient when it came to jailing Rhona Heaney; she was sentenced to 10 years in prison for the conspiracy. Although her husband Jano was acquitted of any involvement in the crime, Irene eventually confessed to being guilty of murder after spending months in denial. In accordance with Australian law at the time, she received the maximum jail sentence of 15 years.

Irene Maslin has since served her time and has been released from prison. Despite her distinct lack of remorse, nothing could prevent her from being allowed back into the general public. Although her current whereabouts are unknown, her reputation has lived on. The barbarism of her action attracted plenty of media attention, and she has been featured on a number of true crime television shows throughout the years. But perhaps the biggest impact she has made lies deep in the hearts of those that were once close to her. Years after the crime, locals still recall the chills she sent shivering down the spines of her neighbors. Some authorities even likened the magnitude of her evil to infamous serial killer Charles Manson.

With Maslin having assumed a new identity, it's almost impossible to know for certain what drove her lust for blood. Perhaps she was genuinely concerned for the safety of Karen Randall; others hypothesize that Paul Snabel's drug habit may have landed him in debt. Irene may have just been seeking the adrenaline high that comes with taking a life. While her motives cannot be conclusively determined, there is an age old lesson to be learned from the tragedy that unfolded in Mirboo North. Though Irene Maslin appeared to be nothing more than an innocent housewife to some, in reality, she was capable committing savage acts – proving that sometimes, the people we hold in the highest regard turn out to be the people we know the least.

THE MURDER FACTORY : THE TRUE STORY AMY ARCHER GILLIGAN

JACK DOYLE

Amy E. Duggan was born in Milton, Connecticut in October of 1868. She was the eighth of ten children born to James Duggan and Mary Kennedy. The Duggan family lived in a middle-class neighborhood, occupying a simple two-story house on Saw Mill Road. Milton, a suburb of Litchfield, was much like any other small, New England town.

Some sources have suggested a history of mental illness in the Duggan family, although very little documentation exists from this era concerning the family. According to the book, "Chronicles of Milton: Village Left Behind by Time," published in 1997 by members of the Milton Women's Club, one of Amy's brothers was said to play the violin all day while standing in front of a mirror, possibly as a result of some sort of psychological condition or mental illness. The book also contains anecdotal reports from the Milton community suggesting that one of Amy's sisters was disabled as a result of either falling or jumping from a window on the second story of the family home. Little information exists concerning her seven other siblings.

A clearer picture of Amy Duggan, who would later become Amy Archer-Gilligan, might emerge given greater insight into her upbringing. Unfortunately, very little is known concerning her early formative years and the circumstances of her childhood. Recordkeeping in the early 20th century, prior to the advent of computerized networks, was far less efficient than it is today.

Concerning Amy's education, it is known that she attended the Milton School for the duration of her early academic career. In 1890, she continued, enrolling in the New Britain Normal School. There is little record of her academic career, although she never received any formal degree or certificate pertaining to elder care, which would ultimately become her career.

In 1897, Amy married James Archer and gave birth to a daughter, Mary, in December of that year. Four years later, in 1901, James and Amy Archer relocated to Newington, Connecticut. They began working as caretakers for an aging widower named John Seymour. The Archers moved into Seymour's home, lived there, and provided care for the elderly man up until his death in 1904. Scant evidence exists concerning this relationship, but the available information indicates that the rapport between the Archers and Seymour was not marked by anything illicit. It is generally believed that his death was not premature, although it is difficult to be certain. Some people have suggested that John Seymour may have been Amy's first true victim, although she was never charged nor convicted of murder in relation to Seymour, and this is generally not assumed to be the case.

Following his death, Mr. Seymour's family converted his former residence into a boarding house for the elderly. The Seymour family rented the building to the Archers, who took in new patients and continued on as professional caregivers. The home was called Sister Amy's Nursing Home for the Elderly. The nickname "Sister Amy" stuck, and it followed Amy throughout the remainder of career and into infamy.

In 1907, three years after opening the boarding house, the Seymour family opted to sell the building. This transition prompted the Archers to move from Newington to Windsor, Connecticut. Amy and James opened another nursing home in Windsor. The location the selected was a 3-story brick building, which they called the Archer Home for Aged People. The couple had saved enough money to buy the building and open the business, but the expenses associated with running maintaining the practice would prove to be a continual struggle. Financial insecurity, it would seem, was a trigger for Amy Archer; a pitfall that she would kill to avoid.

Although Amy was never officially charged with his murder, many have suggested that, in all likelihood, her first husband was her first true victim. James Archer suffered from kidney failure and died, reportedly of natural causes, in 1910. Many have noted, in retrospect, however, that Amy took out a life insurance on her husband just a few weeks prior to his death and that the onset of his ailment was both sudden and unprecedented. At the time it occurred, however, Archer's death was not viewed as suspicious in any way. Whatever the circumstances surrounding his death, natural causes or, as later evidence would suggest, not-so-natural, the money from the insurance policy enabled "Sister Amy" to continue running the Archer Home for Aged People.

At this point, after three years of running the Archer Home, Amy had firmly established herself within the Windsor community as an upstanding citizen. She was active in local affairs, and even donated a stained-glass window to the local church, which she attended on a regular basis. Her reputation was that of a good Christian, and a woman who was content to devote her life to caring for the elderly while making a modest living. In fact, the Archer Home served as a model facility whose influence impacted the development of institutionalized elder care in America, despite the "fatal flaw" in Amy's business model. Investigative journalist M. William Phelps has referred to Amy as a, "Pioneer of elderly care at the turn of the century in New England."

Indeed, Sister Amy was, in her own way, an entrepreneur in the field of elder care. She was among the first to develop what we now commonly think of as assisted-living facilities. It was Amy, ironically, who really introduced the concept of "nursing" into what we now call "nursing homes." Her business savvy coupled with the image she projected of a warm, church-going, nurse who cared for the aging, had clients lining up to enroll in the Archer Home. She marketed herself very successfully, and her entrepreneurial mindset grasped the concepts of supply and demand very astutely. Her methods of maintaining an available supply of beds to meet the demands of patients, however, proved to be quite sinister. Despite her successful business and her apparent obsession with financial security, Amy Archer never seemed to have enough money.

In the summer of 1913, Amy married her second husband, Michael Gilligan, becoming Amy Archer-Gilligan. Michael Gilligan was a wealthy widower with five adult sons of his own who was actually a resident at the Archer Home. He was reportedly interested both in Amy and in investing in the facility that he now called home. It was not long before Amy had lured Mr. Gilligan into a web of seduction, which would prove to have fatal consequences.

Amy was considerably younger than her new husband, although the age difference was not particularly unusual at that time, and their romance seemed, by all appearances, genuine. To the local community, the match seemed, at first, to be perfectly normal.

Their marriage, however, was a short one. Michael Gilligan died after only 3 months of wedlock. On February 19th, 1914, he signed a new will that left the entirety of his estate to his new wife. Less than 48 hours later, he died abruptly of what was determined to be an acute case of "indigestion."

The curious circumstances surrounding Gilligan's death were not seriously investigated at the time, nor were they wholly ignored. The fact that he had completely cut his children out of his will and signed everything he owned over to his new wife was a bit odd, perhaps, but ultimately such things weren't all that unusual; that he died so quickly afterwards, however, raised murmurs of suspicion. It was not until the investigation into Amy Archer-Gilligan was well underway, three years later, that Michael Gilligan's will was shown to be a forgery crafted, of course, by his then-wife. According to some sources, the forged will was written on the very night preceding Gilligan's sudden and untimely demise.

Were it a singular incident, Michael Gilligan's death might have been chalked up to bad luck or coincidence, but 60 people died in the Archer Home between 1907 and 1917, with 48 of those occurring in the 5-year period between 1911 and 1916. Due to the nature of the industry, however, it was some years before local investigators began to ask serious questions about the exorbitantly high death rate coming from the Archer Home.

In the industry of elder care, of course, it is inevitable and expected that patients will eventually die. The ultimate function of a nursing home is precisely to provide end-of-life care to elderly people. It is not as if people "recover" from old age, and this fact was not lost on Amy Archer-Gilligan. Quite the opposite: she relied on the expectation of death associated with elder care as a part of her cover as she "executed" her increasingly dark business plan. Her methods were, no doubt, uncouth, but her business sense was shrewd. She crafted a scheme to take advantage of her vulnerable patients, extort money from them, and conveniently take their lives into her own hands, ending them prematurely when they were no longer providing her with income. Because elderly people were expected to die, she was able to carry out her deeds for years before coming under suspicion.

Part of Amy's scheme involved an up-front payment option available to residents upon entering the facility. Clients who moved into the Archer Home were given the option to pay on a weekly basis or with an up-front payment of $1000, which guaranteed care for the rest of their lives. Many individuals chose the latter option. The sustainability and success of the Archer Home depended on turnover: in the case of up-front payments, once a client had paid they were, in purely economic terms, essentially just taking up space. In order to meet her overhead costs and make a profit, Amy Archer-Gilligan knew that beds would need to be continually available to accommodate new, paying clients. The only problem with this model was, of course, the existing clients. Amy took matters into her own hands.

Within the first four years of the Archer Home, over 20 residents died. While some patient deaths were expected, this was a significantly higher rate than was found in similar establishments. People began to notice. Those clients who paid up-front, in particular, became increasingly notorious for dying suddenly after an alarmingly short time at the Archer Home. In some cases, even those patients who had seemed perfectly healthy succumbed with no warning, seemingly out of nowhere.

Franklin R. Andrews was one such victim. He was a vibrant fellow of sixty-one years with his physical and mental faculties very much intact. On the morning of May 29, 1914, Andrews was working in the garden outside the Archer Home, by all accounts in fine spirits and perfect health. Andrews, a former factory-worker, showed no signs of illness or infirmity as he weeded and watered the flowerbeds outside the house. Within a matter of hours, however, his health suddenly deteriorated at a rapid rate. He was struck with convulsions, horrendous gastro-intestinal distress, and other painful symptoms. By that evening, Andrews was dead. The cause of death was cited, at the time, as a gastric ulcer.

Andrews bequeathed all of his personal affects to his sister, Nellie Pierce. While going through her brother's papers, Pierce found notes referencing several occasions in which Amy Archer-Gilligan had pressed him money, including, at one point, a loan of five-hundred dollars. Pierce became increasingly suspicious. Her brother had been a picture of health, and the contents of his personal papers evoked an uneasy sense that something malicious had occurred in the circumstances surrounding her brother's death. Nellie Pierce reported her findings to the local district attorney, who, at the time, largely ignored her concerns. Who, after all, would suspect a prim, church-going nurse of murdering her elderly patients?

Family members of other residents had also voiced suspicion, however. Despite the district attorney's dismissal of Pierce's concerns, the police were beginning to investigate the matter. Towards the end of 1914, shortly after the death of Frank Andrews, an undercover investigator working with the Connecticut State Police took up residence in the Archer Home posing as a wealthy widow. Her name was Zola Bennet. Bennet used her time as a resident in the house to collect evidence, and she quickly began to see behind the veil of "Sister Amy's" performance as a pious and caring woman. Bennet observed repeated incidents in which the so-called nurse would swindle residents out of large sums of money, valuable possessions, and even property by eliciting sympathy and claiming she was "down on her luck."

Meanwhile, Nellie Pierce remained convinced that something was awry. Having been rebuffed by the district attorney, she took her concerns to the press. *The Hartfourd Courant* picked up the story and journalists began their own investigation of the Archer Home. On May 9, 1916, the newspaper released the first of a series of pieces on the nursing home, which it referred to as the "Murder Factory," and its proprietor, Amy Archer-Gilligan.

The Hartfourd Courant's article series prompted local authorities to take action, and the police launched a more serious investigation into the increasingly infamous "Murder Factory." The investigation was a lengthy process. Forensics, evidence collection, and judicial processes were considerably more primitive in 1916 than in the 21st century, and it took almost a year before police established adequate grounds for the arrest of "Sister Amy."

Amy Archer-Gilligan was a shrewd planner, and she had constructed somewhat of a "backup plan" should she ever come under suspicion. To dispose of her victims, she had enlisted an old mortician to provide regular services to the Archer Home. As soon as a patient died, Amy would rush the body to the mortician to be embalmed. The prompt removal of the bodies, she claimed, was both a matter of efficiency and a gesture done to avoid upsetting the other residents.

The real motive behind her speedy dispatches was in the embalming fluid used by her chosen mortuary. Embalming fluid of this era contained many toxic chemicals, heavy metals, and poisonous substances, including high levels of arsenic.

Arsenic is a naturally occurring chemical element found, into today, in a variety of products, ranging from lead alloys found in ammunition and car batteries to compounds found in wood preservatives and pesticides. Arsenic is still used in numerous industrial contexts, although modern usage is declining. In the 19th century, a green pigment derived from arsenic was used a coloring agent in candies, which resulted in numerous cases of arsenic poisoning. Up until recently, both arsenic and lead were widely used in optical glass.

While high doses of arsenic are poisonous, small doses were used medicinally for centuries. Chinese traditional medicine has used arsenic for over 2,400 years to treat a variety of ailments. During the 18th, 19th, and into the 20th century, arsenic compounds were also used medicinally in the West, in sub-toxic doses, including as a treatment for syphilis. Throughout the Elizabethan era, European women mixed arsenic powder with chalk and vinegar to create a topical anti-aging cream that had a whitening effect on the skin. Undoubtedly, some arsenic entered their bloodstream through the skin, but likely not enough to manifest immediate symptoms of poisoning in most cases.

As a poison, arsenic was used extensively during The Middle Ages and The Renaissance. Symptoms of arsenic poisoning are almost identical to those of cholera, which was prevalent in Europe during those eras. This made arsenic a killing tool of choice, particularly among the elite classes, as arsenic poisoning often became untraceable. Symptoms of severe arsenic poisoning include convulsions, diarrhea, vomiting blood, hair loss, and severe stomach pain. The bodily organs that are typically affected by arsenic poisoning include the lungs, kidneys, skin, and liver. If untreated, acute arsenic poisoning leads rapidly to a coma and death.

In the United States in the early 20th century, during Amy's time, the most common use of arsenic was in rat poison, which was popular and widely accessible at general stores and pharmacies throughout the country. According to Amy, the Archer Home had a serious rat problem. Shopkeepers and townspeople alike took note of Amy's seemingly endless struggle to "kill rats" at the Archer Home. A variety of testimonials revealed that she purchased, over the years, a remarkable amount of rat poison. The paper trail left by Amy's repeated purchases of rat poison, in fact, played a crucial role in her eventual conviction, despite the fact that she took some steps to cover her tracks.

Amy Archer-Gilligan's use of rat poison to kill her patients was difficult to prove precisely, in part, because of her astute choice in morticians. Because the bodies of her victims were immediately transferred to the mortuary and embalmed using fluids that contained the very poisons she had used to commit her crimes, much of the evidence against her was circumstantial, and a proof was difficult to obtain. Forensic technology was still in its early stages at the time, and criminal proceedings moved at a relatively slow pace.

The image she fabricated of a kind, caring woman who served as a nurse to the elderly was successful in deterring a conviction for some time, furthered by her own denials and vehement Bible-thumping. Photographs of Amy Archer-Gilligan from the period following her initial engagement with authorities show a stern woman with prim brown curls. She is dressed in a high-collared shirt with a white ribbon that clings tightly around her neck, a faint smile on her thin lips. Her eyes are bright, but distant, casting an eerie vacancy over her entire image. They seem to betray her otherwise composed appearance, hinting at an unfathomable darkness lurking just below the surface. Despite her best efforts, by 1916 people were beginning to see through her façade.

Several bodies were exhumed during the course of the investigation of Amy Archer-Gilligan, leading up to her initial trial in June of 1917. Authorities found exorbitantly high levels of arsenic in the bodies of multiple residents from the Archer Home and in the body of Amy's second husband, Michael Gilligan. Due to the presence of arsenic in the embalming fluid used to prepare the bodies for burial, however, solid evidence of poisoning was difficult to ascertain at the time.

This difficulty was compounded by Amy's cleverness. She deliberately charged her patients with the task of going to the store to pick up rat poison, thus purchasing it, herself, only on occasion. Of course, many of the residents who went on these excursions to purchase rat poison for the Archer Home ended up becoming Amy's victims themselves, and therefore it took some time for the authorities to assemble the pieces of the puzzle. It was not until authorities thoroughly examined the records of arsenic purchases that they were able to assemble the evidence necessary to make an arrest.

Another important player Amy's web of lies was Dr. King, the physician employed by the Archer Home. Dr. King was responsible for signing off on the death certificates, and determining the cause of death, concerning the bodies coming out of the Archer Home. He was also responsible for several arsenic purchases for the Archer Home. King came under suspicion for a period of time during the investigation into Amy Archer-Gilligan, but as the police began to exhume the bodies of the victims, the focus ultimately fell on Amy.

Franklin Andrews, the brother of Nellie Piece, was the first of the victims to be exhumed. Nearly two years had elapsed since his untimely death, and upon further inspection of his remains a forensic investigation found enough arsenic in his stomach to kill seven full-grown men. Due to the nature of the embalming process, it was clear that the amount of arsenic and its presence in Andrews' stomach were not a result of embalming and could be attributed only to his ingestion of this fatal compound. The only plausible explanation for his death was that he had been poisoned.

The remains of Alice Gowdy, another resident and potential victim, were also unearthed. She and her husband had moved to the Archer Home together in June of 1914, when Alice was sixty-nine years old. Within a few short months, she had died suddenly after experiencing symptoms similar to those that had befallen Andrews. An examination of her body also revealed high levels of arsenic.

Amy's second husband, Michael Gilligan, was the third of her victims to be exhumed. Forensic analysis showed that his body was also loaded with arsenic. At this point, a closer examination of Michael Gilligan's will revealed it as a forgery, clearly written in Amy's handwriting.

A man named Charles Smith was the fourth body that the authorities unearthed for examination. Records indicate that Charles Smith, over the course of two years, turned his entire life-savings over to Amy Archer-Gilligan, totaling over $3000. After the transfer of this sum, he immediately died of what was initially cited as a "stroke" by Dr. King. An examination of his body determined Smith's death was not, in fact, caused by a stroke, but rather due to exposure to toxic levels of arsenic. He was eighty-seven years old when he died.

The remains of thirty-three year old Maude Lynch were the next to come out of the ground. Lynch, a young woman with certain disabilities, had been placed into care at the Archer Home by her family. At the time of her death, Dr. King ruled the causes as being attributed to a form of anemia and epilepsy. A subsequent autopsy found that Ms. Lynch had, in fact, been killed by strychnine poisoning.

Strychnine is a highly toxic alkaloid found in pesticides, notably including rat poison. Like arsenic, people once believed that in sub-toxic doses strychnine possessed medicinal benefits and it was used as a stimulant and athletic performance enhancer throughout the late 19th and early 20th century. Today, no known medicinal value is attributed to strychnine. In toxic doses, strychnine poisoning is known to produce some of the most painful symptoms of any toxic reaction, including extreme spasms and convulsions.

Despite the presence of toxic levels of arsenic and strychnine found in multiple bodies belonging to former residents of the Archer Home who had been under Amy's direct care, the facts were difficult to ascertain. Technicalities made it difficult to prove Amy's guilt in a court of law. Of Amy Archer-Gilligan's 40-plus suspected victims, only the Andrews case ultimately provided sufficient evidence for a jury to convict her of murder. During her initial trial, she was tried for five accounts of murder, but her lawyer got the charges reduced to a single count: the murder of Franklin R. Andrews. On June 18, 1917, after a yearlong investigation, a four-week trial, and four hours of deliberation, a jury found Amy Archer-Gilligan guilty and she was sentenced to death by hanging.

She never confessed to the crime. In fact, Amy appealed her conviction. A technicality caused the initial ruling to be overturned by the proceeding judge, and a new trial was set for 1919. The two years she spent in prison leading up to her second trial appeared to take a toll on Amy's psychological condition. She pleaded insanity at the second trial, and was subsequently found, once again, guilty of murder. This time she was not given a death sentence, but was instead sentenced to spend life in prison.

In 1924, Amy was transferred from prison to the Connecticut Hospital for the Insane in Middletown. The details of the transfer remain unclear, but it is assumed that she suffered some kind of psychotic break while incarcerated that prompted the shift in custody. She remained at the mental hospital until her death on April 23, 1962. She was 89 years old, having spent nearly half of her life incarcerated and institutionalized.

The question of what drives a serial killer to enact such heinous crimes is one that forensics specialists and criminal investigators spend their lives pondering. In some cases, the motivation is apparently perverse sexual desire, as was the case of Jeffery Dahmer; in others, such as David Berkowitz, the so-called "Son of Sam," it was a warped sense of pseudo-religious compulsion. In Amy Archer's case, the motivation was apparently in large part financial, although what ultimately drove her to kill remains a mystery.

In Amy's second trial, in 1919, her daughter, Mary Archer, testified that her mother was addicted to the powerful opiate morphine, which is similar to heroin both in effect and addictive capacity. At the time, the court did not seem particularly interested in exploring a correlation between her alleged drug addiction and her criminal behavior. It is quite possible, however, that her relationship with the highly addictive narcotic could have had a significant impact on her behavior. Morphine addicts often suffer from severe psychological dependence on the drug, depression, amnesia, paranoia, and an array of other symptoms that often lead to substantial mental health issues. Skeptics have argued that Amy's claim of morphine addiction was fabricated to help her case, and there is no evidence to support or refute her alleged drug use. Furthermore, it is impossible to gauge, if she was, in fact, addicted to morphine, whether or not this contributed to her murderous behavior; and if so, to what extent.

The investigation and trial of Amy Archer-Gilligan received national attention from the press at the time, and the "Murder House" became a place of infamy. The story, itself, achieved a certain level of notoriety simply due to its bizarre nature and the shock surrounding "Sister Amy" and her true persona. Perhaps even more famous than Amy Archer-Gilligan, herself, however, was the successful Broadway Show and subsequent Hollywood movie that her story inspired.

In the late 1930's a New York playwright named Joseph Kesselring became interested in the story of Amy Archer-Gilligan. After reading about her, Kesselring took it upon himself to bring the bizarre tale of America's first female serial killer to the stage. He traveled to Connecticut to conduct research on her case, and then he began to work on adapting the events into a Broadway show. What transpired took the form of dark comedy, called "Arsenic and Old Lace," which was loosely based on Amy Archer-Gilligan and her Murder House.

Kesselring took numerous artistic liberties with the story, perhaps most notable converting Amy from a singular character into a pair of quirky sisters, Abby and Martha Brewster. These two seemingly benign ladies would poison their male guests with arsenic mixed into elderberry wine and bury their bodies in the basement of their house. The sisters claim, during the course of the performance, that the murders are an "act of charity." They believed they are doing a service by ending the lives of elderly gentlemen that they presume are suffering due to loneliness and infirmity. There is no evidence to suggest that the real Amy Archer-Gilligan had any illusions of charity when she poisoned her unsuspecting victims.

"Arsenic and Old Lace" opened on Broadway in 1941 and enjoyed a successful three-year run. The play was later adapted into a film, directed by Frank Capra. The film rendition of "Arsenic and Old Lace" stars Cary Grant in the role of Mortimer Brewster, one of two nephews of Abby and Martha. Mortimer, who is newly engaged, discovers a body in the house belonging to his aunts and subsequently makes increasingly feverish attempts to prevent further murders from taking place while simultaneously shifting the blame onto Teddy, the mentally unstable brother of Abby and Martha.

Teddy's impairment is defined by his being convinced that he is actually Teddy Roosevelt, which at the time of the original stage production was considered savvy political humor. Originally Bob Hope was slotted for the role of Mortimer, but his contract with Paramount prohibited him from participating in the film. It is likely that Kesselring had heard rumors concerning the history of mental illness in the Duggan family during the course of his research into Amy Archer-Gilligan's past, which he then incorporated into the plotline of his adaption. Cary Grant's character, Mortimer, famously tells his fiancé in the film, "Insanity runs in my family, practically gallops!" The character of Teddy, Mortimer's brother, Jonathon, and the murderous sisters, Abby and Martha, are all portrayed as mentally unsound in varying capacities.

Many have speculated that the popularity of both the stage play and later screen production of the tale were attributed to the atmosphere of the early 1940's, set against the backdrop of World War II. With so much death and violence going on at the time, the ability to incorporate humor into otherwise macabre situations was something that appealed to many viewers of the era. Both the play and film became classics, with stage versions being performed in theaters into contemporary times.

The popularity and success of "Arsenic and Old Lace" over a period of decades meant that the story eventually reached audiences that had likely never heard of the real woman who served as the film's inspiration. At the same time, it has also played a role in ensuring that the story of Amy Archer-Gilligan has never quite faded into obscurity.

The dubious details of the case of Amy Archer-Gilligan still hold a certain fascination. Is it possible that she was innocent? She never confessed. Perhaps she really did have a rat problem? Could the presence of arsenic in embalming fluid and the errors associated with early forensic technology have steered the course of the investigation in the wrong direction? Is it possible that, perhaps, those people really did die of natural causes? The New York Times published an article in 1997 raising these very questions. All things considered, it is unlikely that Amy Archer-Gilligan's reputation as a villainous murderer is unwarranted. The signs point to her, and experts generally agree that she was responsible for the deaths of at least five people, and possibly as many as 60.

The Archer Home (or "Murder House") still stands in Windsor, Connecticut at 37 Prospect St, not far from the center of town. Like other large houses in the neighborhood, it has been converted into an unassuming complex of apartment buildings. Passing by the building today, one would never guess that it was once home to what was almost certainly one of America's most prolific female serial killers.